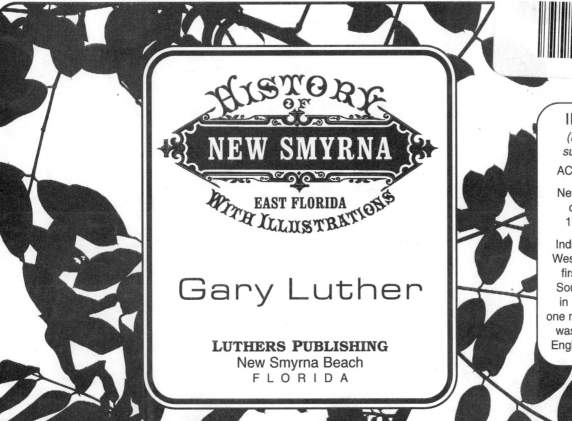

HISTORY OF NEW SMYRNA

EAST FLORIDA

WITH ILLUSTRATIONS

Gary Luther

LUTHERS PUBLISHING

New Smyrna Beach

F L O R I D A

INDIGO

(Indigofera suffruticosa)

ACTUAL SIZE

New Smyrna's cash crop 1769–1777

Indigo from the West Indies was first grown in South Carolina in 1742. Over one million pounds was shipped to England in 1775.

PRINTED IN THE UNITED STATES OF AMERICA

Published by
LUTHERS PUBLISHING
1009 NORTH DIXIE FREEWAY
NEW SMYRNA BEACH, FL 32168-6221
www.lutherspublishing.com

LIBRARY OF CONGRESS
CATALOGING-IN-PUBLICATION DATA
Luther, Gary. 1947–. 1st ed.
History of New Smyrna, east Florida:
with illustrations/Gary Luther.
p.   cm.
Includes bibliographical references.
ISBN 1-877633-61-5 (pbk.)
1. New Smyrna Beach (Fla.)—History—Miscellanea.
2. New Smyrna Beach (Fla.)—History—Pictorial works.
I. Title.

F319.N5 L88 2001
975.9'21—dc21   200103855

Ponce de Leon
Inlet jetties
Photo by Bill Ficklin

TABLE OF CONTENTS

EDITORIAL COLUMN.....................4

FLORIDA GEOGRAPHY
AND GEOLOGY..........................8

ORIGINS OF COQUINA.................9

MEET THE INDIANS...................10

TURTLE MOUND........................13

**FIRST SPANISH
PERIOD (1565–1763)**...........16

PONCE DE LEON'S BATTLE.......17

PEDRO SLEPT HERE.................19

**BRITISH COLONIAL
PERIOD (1763–1783)**...........21

DR. TURNBULL'S
GREATEST VENTURE...............22

TURNBULL'S EXPERIMENT........24

RIDE THE KING'S ROAD............25

DR. & MRS. TURNBULL.............26

BIBLICAL SMYRNA...................27

BARTRAM NOTES....................29

MAP OF MINORCA..................30

COLONISTS & PIRATES............31

THIS INDENTURE.....................32

DID 500 SLAVES PERISH?.........33

CANAL STREET NAME.............34

1768 REBELLION....................36

TURNBULL'S COW-PEN............39

FALL OF NEW SMYRNA............40

**SECOND SPANISH PERIOD
(1783-1821)**...................43

THE ROCK HOUSE...................45

OLD FORT PARK: 1805
HOUSE ON THE HILL...............47

1817 SURVEY MAP.................50

**FLORIDA TERRITORY &
STATEHOOD (1821–1845)**.....52

FORT NEW SMYRNA.................53

DUNHAM MANSION..................55

NEW SMYRNA ABLAZE............56

MASSACRE BLUFF..................58

SUGAR MILL ORIGINS.............59

BRONZE CANDLESTICKS.........62

MISSION MYTH......................63

SKIRMISH AT THE
OLD STONE WHARF.................66

TRAGEDY OF WAR..................68

BURIED RIFLES?.....................71

BURNED AND BOMBED............72

SHELDON HOUSE
AT OLD FORT PARK................74

DOWNTOWN 1888.................79

FIRST TRAIN ARRIVES.............80

FEC RAILWAY.......................81

CITY COUNCIL'S MINUTES.......84

MAYOR'S COURT...................90

"CITY GATES".......................93

FIRST SCHOOL.....................94

SECOND/THIRD SCHOOL.........95

ROOM 1 CLASS PHOTO.........96

EARLY CANAL STREET.............97

CANAL STREET.....................98

CANAL ST./NEW MUSEUM........99

1924 FLOOD.......................100

HOTELS.............................101

BOATS ON THE RIVER.............102

NORTH BRIDGE....................103

SOUTH BRIDGE....................105

CORONADO BEACH................106

RIVERVIEW HOTEL................108

DUMMETT'S GRAVE...............110

ATLANTIC HOUSE..................111

CASINO/FLAGLER RAMP.........112

FISHING.............................113

MANTA RAY & TURTLE............114

STRAY WHALES...................115

CAR & SURF DON'T MIX..........116

SURF'S UP!.........................117

ON THE BEACH....................118

BEACH SCENES...................119

WRECKED HERE...................120

TREASURE HUNTING.............123

FIRST LIGHTHOUSE...............125

PONCE LIGHTHOUSE.............126

BIBLIOGRAPHY....................128

IS NEW SMYRNA OLDER THAN ST. AUGUSTINE?

Every story has a beginning. Here's the origin for the belief that New Smyrna was the site of the first St. Augustine and therefore is the oldest US city:

"Location of the original St. Augustine is not known. Its ancient site can no longer be determined, but it is known it did not command the entrance of the harbor, and was much exposed to the attacks of Indians. When, in May of the following year [nine months later, 1566], the settlement was moved to a more advantageous position, the first location received the name of Old St. Augustine from the Spaniards." — Woodbury Lowery, *The Spanish Settlements: 1513–1561,* published in 1901.

Would merely moving across town discourage hostile Indians? Ponce de Leon was attacked by Indians in our area in 1513. The site of New Smyrna is down the river and around a bend. It has no view of the inlet.

Recall the official St. Augustine slogan. You might suspect a lawyer carefully crafted this language: "The Oldest Continuously Inhabited City in the United States."

OLD MAPS SHOW ANOTHER INLET

Several maps from 1564 through 1774 show an inlet north of Cape Canaveral and south of Ponce de Leon Inlet.

Our beachside is actually a barrier island. The narrowest point between our inlet and Cape Canaveral occurs in the 24-mile Canaveral National Seashore.

Within the past century, a washover between the ocean and Indian River North occurred near the last parking lot (number five), once the site of the Mosquito Lagoon Coast Guard Station and House of Refuge.

This created a shallow, temporary "inlet." Of course, the counting and naming of inlets by map makers may have been further confused by this additional feature.

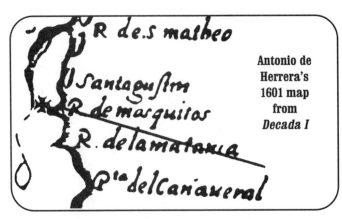

Antonio de Herrera's 1601 map from Decada I

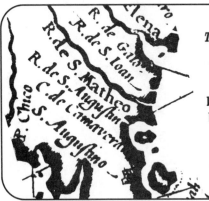

Americae Tabula Nova Multis. Published in 1601. This copy was acquired from the Library of Congress by John Y. Detwiler in 1924. Today the map is in the New Smyrna Historical Museum archives.

BEFUDDLED HISTORIAN OR HIDDEN TRUTH?

Antonio de Herrera (1559-1625) was appointed official historiographer in 1592 by King Philip II of Spain. This position allowed Herrera access to original and secret papers for publishing the history of the West Indies, *Decada I,* in 1601. Herrera offers the only account from Ponce de Leon's personal log or perhaps a report to the King regarding the discovery of Florida. These documents have long since been lost or destroyed.

Geographical information on the West Indies was a state secret, deposited in the Casa de Contratación (Royal House of Trade) in Seville. As early as 1511, it was forbidden to supply foreigners with charts or maps without license from the King. Even crews of vessels sailing to the West Indies excluded foreigners.

Despite all of his "insider" information, Herrera had difficulty identifying inlets, placing Matanzas Inlet north of Cape Canaveral and south of our inlet. For some reason, Mosquito Inlet (renamed Ponce de Leon in 1927) was marked prominently with a Maltese cross. Does this indicate 29° north latitude or perhaps "Old" St. Augustine?

Was Herrera revealing some forgotten knowledge in this map? Or was it disinformation? A variation of the "confused" location of inlets is continued in *Americae Tabula Nova Multis,* published in 1601.

THE UNRELIABLE, INACCURATE NAVIGATOR MYTH

Data from early navigators has often been dismissed because of their crude instruments. However, sailing by latitude (east-west) was sufficiently well understood that most crews who arrived in the New World managed to find their way home to Europe.

Computation of latitude was discussed in illustrated navigation books by Alvise Cá da Mosto, 1490; Pietro Maritire d'Anghiera, 1504; Francisco Faleiro, 1535; and Martin Cortes, 1561. Determining longitude didn't occur until accurate chronometers were perfected in the 1750's.

Let's assume latitude accuracy no greater than a quarter of a degree (15 nautical miles). Why? In 1573, Pedro Menendez Marques (page 19) noted Cape Canaveral at 28° and a quarter (28.250°). The actual measurement is 28.458°, which Marques under-estimated by 12.5 nautical miles.

St. Augustine Inlet is at 29.910° N, *within 5.4 nautical miles from being exactly 30°.*

Our Ponce de Leon Inlet (Mosquito Inlet until 1927) is at 29.072° N, *within 4.3 nautical miles from being exactly 29° N.*

Therefore, early navigators would have recorded St. Augustine in 30° and Mosquito Inlet in 29° because they couldn't accurately measure such a slight difference.

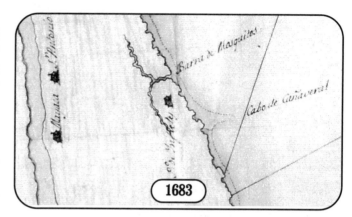

1683

1715

SPANISH MISSIONS AND WHAT'S ALLAWATA?

Alonzo Solano's 1683 map (left) includes a symbol for a church west of our inlet (Barre de Mosquitos). Maps from 1715, 1733 and 1774 show similar symbols with the notation "Allawata," which sounds like an Indian word. An Internet search shows "Allawatah" is a town in Tunisia and "Al Hawwata" is in Sudan.

Certainly the remains of a coquina sugar mill exist today at Mission Drive and Old Mission Road. Indeed, Indians set fire to it in 1835. However, this was a work-a-day sugar mill. Would most entrepreneurs spend extra money for graceful arches? The least expensive "construction" would be to modify an existing structure.

While coquina was available, it was most easily recycled from another building. After all, is it easier to quarry stone or cut timber? Some sugar mills were made of wood. Others have suggested that coquina was used because it was fireproof. What about the roof? When the Indians set fire to the Sugar Mill, what burned?

The 1733 Henry Popple map (right) is courtesy (plus $35) of the Texas State Library & Archives Commission. This is its first publication in any local historical work. "Allawata" is shown on our mainland. The two structures on the beachside barrier island look like houses, unlike the notation for trees or Indian mounds.

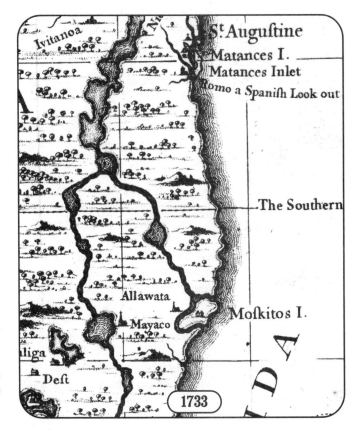

A QUICK LESSON IN FLORIDA GEOGRAPHY AND GEOLOGY

When the first American Indians entered Florida some 12,000 years ago, the sea level was as much as 350 feet lower than today. Originally, Florida's western shoreline extended over 100 miles farther into the Gulf of Mexico. The climate was cooler and drier; the Indians hunted mastodon, mammoth, horse, camel, bison, and giant land tortoises.

As the glaciers melted, Florida became wetter. By 9,000 B.C., the sea rose and flooded the coastal areas. The climate continued to warm until 3,000 B.C., when the weather began to resemble present day conditions.

Geologically, our beautiful white sand is due to titanium dioxide (TiO_2) mixed with regular sand (SiO_2). The sand packs hard, making it ideal for driving. High speed film is not needed on this brilliant white beach.

The 1940's slogan "The World's Safest Beach" is loosely based on the fact our shoreline slopes gradually. It is 40 feet deep at 15 miles out and 600 feet at 50 miles. "Safest" is just a shameful advertising myth still repeated. Heads up! Volusia County beaches hold the world's record for shark bites, with one fatality in 1981.

Florida's East Coast as seen by the ERTS-1 satellite from 560 miles altitude. Cape Canaveral is featured at the bottom right. To the top within 3/8" is Ponce de Leon Inlet.

The largest lakes closest to the Cape (clockwise) are Lake Harney, Lake Jessup, Lake Monroe, and Lake Ashby. Florida's East Coast doesn't run exactly north and south, but more NNW to SSE (or like the clock hands at 5:50). Those white cotton puff balls are the tops of clouds. (Photo courtesy of NASA)

Coquina is a limestone composed of thousands of periwinkle shells cemented together with calcite. This sedimentary rock was formed during the Pleistocene epoch (Ice Age) one million years ago.

If you thought Florida was made only of sand, think again. The woodcut above illustrates coquina quarrying on Anastasia Island, St. Augustine in 1872. This shellstone only occurs along Florida's East Coast from St. Johns to Palm Beach counties, usually not more than three miles inland. It is also found in New Zealand.

St. Augustine's fort Castillo de San Marcos, begun in 1672, was built of coquina. It was also used in New Smyrna's Sugar Mill, Rock House, Old Stone Wharf, Old Fort Park foundations, wells, and for lining the walls in Turnbull's canal system.

Watching television news as it happens is a common occurrence today. Europeans waited 27 years for their first view of Florida's Indians. Jacques Le Moyne de Morgues' original sketches of his 1564 voyage were published by the Flemish engraver Theodore de Bry in 1591.

UP CLOSE AND PERSONAL: LET'S MEET THE LOCAL INDIANS

Father Francisco Pareja lived among the Timucuan Indians for 33 years. He arrived in Florida on September 23, 1595, to teach them a new religion—Christianity. Father Pareja converted over 500 Indians. His book, *Confessionario*, was published in 1613. It provides a glimpse into their tribal customs and superstitions.

◆ A singing woodpecker meant to keep quiet or risk a nosebleed. A blue jay's song meant someone was coming or something important was about to happen. Of course, an owl was plainly an evil portent.

◆ Whistling at sandbars or obstacles in choppy waters would ensure that your canoe would not capsize. Whistling against a storm could make it stop.

◆ The dreams and words of people possessed were taken as truth.

◆ Lightning and popping of coals in a fire were certain signs of war.

◆ Competitive games were very popular. However, some Indians lied, scored improperly (in their favor), while others took herbs to improve their athletic abilities.

◆ The sorcerer always got his due, blessing and sharing in the first fruits of the harvest. Before fishing, the chief arranged for prayers to the waters. The first fish was caught, smoked over the fire, and half was given to the sorcerer who had conducted the ritual.

◆ Only the chief could have more than one wife. At marriage ceremonies, a sorcerer prayed over the couple. If they didn't pay, he would threaten couple with various forms of marital unhappiness. Sometimes the sorcerer would threaten the debtor with death—or in less severe cases, with rupture, wounded legs or feet. In any event, he could kill anyone with a concoction of poisonous snake, black snake skins, black Spanish moss, and a few unspecified herbs.

◆ Love magic existed. A sorcerer could attract a woman by using special herbs. He could also entice her from a house by singing a spell.

◆ When suicides occurred, the method was usually poisoning or hanging.

◆ Women believed herbal perfumes sprinkled on their skimpy Spanish moss garments would attract men—or prevent their own husbands from straying. Bathing with other herbs would return those husbands who had already wandered.

◆ Meeting a snake on a path, in the field or in your house was an evil omen.

◆ Abortions—especially in extramarital affairs—were common and accomplished by drinking herbs, or by a sharp blow or strong pressure to "choke" the fetus.

◆ Applying the juice of a certain herb to your body before battle was believed to prevent arrow wounds.

◆ Adult or child, eating pottery, charcoal, dirt, lice, or fleas was common. Archaeologists later explained that the Indians frequently ate bugs, worms, roots—even dirt or clay—when their normal food supply was disrupted.

◆ Of course, acorn cakes were more popular than the above entry. The Indian recipe was simple: Remove hulls from the acorn meats. Grind well; bury in warm-to-hot sand. Remove; sprinkle with boiling water until the dough is cooked into a loaf.

◆ After a meal of oysters, clams and acorn cakes, belching might be expected. Belching could go either way: it foretold plenty to eat or death.

◆ Finally, most accounts describe the Timucuans as tall, handsome, athletic, and well-formed. The most prominent were tattooed. Those devoted to high fashion wore dyed fish bladder ornaments.

Men wore their hair pulled into top-knots, often decorated with reeds and plumes. But the secret ingredient in all successful coiffures was bear grease, which was also good for warding off mosquitoes.

Indian artifacts from the Sams' collection, 1925

Excavation of the South Canal shell mound about 1900

TURTLE MOUND:
THE FIRST FLORIDIANS' LEGACY

The Indians were here first. This area was inhabited by nomadic hunters and gathers beginning about 12,000 years ago. Their sand burial mounds and shell mounds (kitchen middens or refuse heaps) dot Florida's coastline.

Surruque Indians, part of the Timucuan tribe living in northern and central Florida, "built" Turtle Mound which is within Canaveral National Seashore, seven miles south of New Smyrna Beach on A1A.

Dr. Amos W. Butler's "Observations on Some Shell Mounds on the Eastern Coast of Florida," published in 1917, identifies 22 shell mounds from Ponce Inlet to Oak Hill. With the exception of the Rock House Mound and the South Canal site, all were created after 500 B.C. with the most inhabitation after 800 A.D.

Unfortunately, nearly all the mounds he recorded were used as handy sources of roadbed fill in the early 1900's. Turtle Mound was saved from a similar fate in 1924 when it was purchased by the Florida State Historical Society for $8,000. One of few survivors, it is the largest on the Florida East Coast and is now part of the National Park Service's Canaveral National Seashore.

The shell mound builders were not as fortunate. Within 200 years of Ponce de Leon's landing on these shores, the entire Timucuan population had disappeared. Some were taken as slaves, but most succumbed to European infections.

A "Columbian exchange" of diseases resulted from two isolated cultures meeting. According to this theory, Europeans brought measles, malaria and smallpox to the New World. Indians gave the explorers the "Great Pox"—syphilis—in this pathogenic exchange.

Turtle Mound contains approximately 33,000 cubic yards of oyster shell, extends 600 feet along the eastern shore of the Indian River, covers two acres, and is about 50 feet high. It has been used as a navigational aid from the days of the earliest Spanish explorers.

Such mounds served the Indians in many ways: refuse disposal, lookouts and signal posts, objects of veneration, and elevated campsites that offered some relief from the ubiquitous sand fleas and mosquitoes. The strata of shell mounds record habitation at intervals over hundreds of years, with progressive layers of food remains, animal bones, charcoal, and broken pottery.

From these "kitchen" remains archaeologists know the Indian diet consisted of mostly shellfish, but included mullet, snook, shark, deer, raccoon, opossum, rabbit, and sometimes even alligator. Indian burials and related objects are not usually found in the shell mounds. Sand mounds associated with the larger shell mounds served that purpose.

Jacques Le Moyne's 1564 map shows Turtle Mound as "Sorrochos." Ponce de Leon Inlet is "F. Sorrochos."

In 1605 Captain Alvaro Mexia was sent to explore the East Florida waterways and to make contact with its different tribes. His report to Spanish Governor Ybarra in St. Augustine noted:

"The river pursues its way to the southeast, all through mangrove islands and sand mounds and palmetto groves and hillocks of low evergreen, oaks on its east bank. It makes many twists, and passes the foot of the mound which they call the 'Mound of Surruque.' This is a hill of oyster shell and short grass, and at the foot of the said hill the Indians of Surruque launch their canoes and go to sea."

Mexia's 1605 reconnaissance map is the earliest detailed view of our inlet and waterways. The site of Turtle Mound is marked with a cross and the notation "Baradero de Suroc." This translates to a shipyard or place where the Surruque kept their canoes or dugouts made from oak and cypress logs.

Turtle Mound is so named because its silhouette

resembles a giant turtle from sea. Contrary to one inland newspaper's account, Turtle Mound is not "composed largely of turtle shells." It is an accumulation of centuries of oyster and clam shells from generations of meals.

Through the years it has had several other names:

SORROCHOS, 1564
BARADERO DE SUROC, 1605
LA ROQUE, 1763
MOUNT BELVEDERE, 1766
MOUNT TURTLE, 1774
MOUNT VELVIDERE, 1796
MOUNT TUCKER, 1796
TURTLE MOUND, 1823.

Today, visitors to this historic site within Canaveral National Seashore can enjoy a memorable prospect of both the ocean and river. Wooden ramps and walkways make it accessible for all.

Unique foliage abounds, including sweet bay, blindwood, Cherokee bean, ground cherry, Virginia creeper, wild cucumber, wild coffee shrubs, shoestring fern, goldenrod, sea grape, turtle grass, wild heliotrope, ironwood, marine ivy, cherry laurel, moonflower, French mulberry, sea myrtle, sour orange, passion flower, sweet bay, sea purslane, resurrection fern, marsh rosemary, beach sunflower and other species for the astute observer to discover. In doubt? Ask a park ranger.

Panoramic river view from atop Turtle Mound

Turtle Mound as seen by boat in the Indian River North

First Spanish Period 1565 – 1763

PONCE DE LEON BATTLED INDIANS HERE IN 1513

Juan Ponce de Leon was an experienced trans-Atlantic explorer; he had accompanied Columbus on his second voyage in 1493.

After "pacifying" Puerto Rico—using greyhounds to hunt Indians who did not submit to his authority—he was rewarded with governorship of the island. His technique of hunting Indians with dogs led to a new Spanish word, *aperrear*, meaning "to cast to the dogs."

But all his land, gold and slaves paled beside the rumored "Fountain of Youth." Commanding three vessels, he first passed the Bahamas, sailed northwest where he sighted an unknown land which he believed to be an island. He named this land "Florida," as a chronicler of the event wrote, "because it appeared delightful, having many pleasant groves" and because it was *Pasqua de Flores* (Feast of the Resurrection or Flowers) during Easter season.

They remained offshore for six days during the first week of April 1513. Ponce went ashore to gain information and to take possession of the land.

Sailing south, his ships met a strong current—the

This woodcut is from the 1726 English edition of Antonio de Herrera's (1559-1625) comprehensive history of early Spanish exploration in the New World, *Decada I*, first published in 1601.

The illustration features Juan Ponce watching his men battle 60 Indians near New Smyrna. Ponce's three ships can be seen sailing south, with his men engaged in a battle south of an inlet where he left an inscribed hewn cross of stone. He named it "La Cruz" (the Cross), later renamed Mosquito Inlet.

This inlet is our present day Ponce de Leon Inlet. The land jutting out into the Atlantic Ocean, occupied by Indians with bows and arrows, is Cape Canaveral.

Gulf Stream—which swept one vessel (a brigantine) out of sight. The other two ships anchored. The Indians on shore hailed Ponce de Leon.

What happened next was recorded by Antonio de Herrera in *Decada I*, a monumental history of Spain's New World colonization efforts, published in 1601:

"Here Juan Ponce went on shore, called by the Indians, who immediately tried to take the boat, the oars and arms. And not to break with them they suffered them, and in order not to alarm the land.

"But because they struck a seaman with a stick, from which he remained unconscious, they had a fight with them who with their arrows and armed staves, the points of sharpened bones and fish spines, wounded two Spaniards, and the Indians received little harm.

"The night separated them, Juan Ponce regathered the Spaniards after hard work. He departed there to a river where he took water and firewood, and was awaiting the brigantine.

"Sixty Indians ran there to hinder him. He took one of them for a pilot, so that he might learn the language. He gave this river the name La Cruz and he left, in it, one of hewn stone with an inscription; they did not finish taking water because it was brackish."

"Rio de la Cruz" translates to "River of the Cross." It gains its name from the stone cross left by Juan Ponce, but it also describes the intersection of our Inlet, Spruce Creek or Rock House Creek, and the Halifax River and the Indian River North, which roughly form a cross.

Is Rio de la Cruz the same as our Ponce de Leon Inlet? King Philip II of Spain certainly thought so. "Report on French Settlement in Florida" by Manrique de Rojas in 1564 connects our inlet to Rio de La Cruz as well as to the failed French attempt to claim Florida.

Rojas advised King Philip II that French Huguenot Captain Jean Ribaut had set up two stone columns bearing the arms of France in Spanish Florida. King Philip sent explicit orders to the Governor of Cuba who on April 29, 1564, assigned them to the Captain of a Spanish frigate. The King's directions are clear:

"Having gone out of this harbor [Havana]...you will enter the Bahama Channel and sail along the Florida coast until you arrive at the shore of La Cruz which is in the twenty-ninth parallel of latitude. There you will land men to seek a stone column or marker bearing the arms of France, which is set up there. Having found it you will remove it and destroy it, or if it proves to be a thing that can be transported in the frigate, you will bring it with you."

LATITUDE, LONGITUDE AND NAUTICAL MILES

PONCE DE LEON INLET: 29.072° N, 80.919° W

ST. AUGUSTINE: 29.910° N, 81.290° W
53.92 nautical miles north of Ponce de Leon Inlet
CAPE CANAVERAL: 28.458° N, 80.533° W
42.09 nautical miles south of Ponce de Leon Inlet
(One nautical mile equals 6,076 feet.)

PEDRO MENENDEZ MARQUES SLEPT HERE...IN 1573

Menendez Marques sailed eight years after his uncle Don Pedro Menendez de Aviles founded St. Augustine in 1565. Marques' four vessels with 150 soldiers were reconnoitering the east coast of Florida. He entered our inlet and probably anchored in the deep channel, north of the North Causeway bridge.

Here is a portion of his account: "Pedro Menendez Marques, Governor of Florida, lacked a cosmographer, wherefore he could not make a map or chart, being compelled to sail along, writing all that could lead to a special knowledge of the east coast of Florida toward the north in such wise that without much trouble it could afterward be made out and charted," Marques recorded in a manuscript cataloged

High beach dunes at the inlet, 1939 photo by N.L. Swartout

as *A Fragment of the Description of the Voyage of Pedro Menendez Marques Along the East Coast of Florida in 1573.*

"The cape of Canaveral is in 28 degrees and a quarter, and ten leagues therefrom is the bar of Mosquitos."

The "bar of Mosquitos" still exists at Ponce de Leon Inlet (called Mosquito Inlet until 1927).

The distance of a Spanish "league" varied from 2.67 to 3.3 nautical miles. Marques was judging distance by dead reckoning, an estimate based on his previous observations. While today's distance from Cape Canaveral to Ponce de Leon Inlet is 42 nautical miles, Marques' estimate of 10 leagues is short. He didn't account for the strength of the northerly Gulf Stream current. Consequently, every distance Marques reported during his journey from the Florida Keys to Cape Hatteras was consistently underestimated.

Marques found our inlet "at ebb tide has a depth of

Jacques Le Moyne's sketch from his ill-fated 1564 voyage depicts a fortified Indian village and their use of weirs to trap fish. This technique was described in 1573 by Pedro Menendez Marques while reconnoitering our inlet and river.

two varas and a half [7.95 feet]. There are sand dunes north and south. He entered east and west, by a very narrow entrance wherefore he came to the sand dune on the north, and the shoal on the starboard [north].

"Once within, he went to the port side [south], because the river could be sounded, and was unnavigatable to the south."

This appears contradictory. Depending upon the tides and the size of his ship, the river farther south may have been too shallow because of exposed shoals or sand bars. For whatever reason, Marques did not attempt to navigate farther south.

"He came to a high sand dune on the port side showing the beginning of a grove where there are some fish weirs, and there he anchored." This would be New Smyrna's north beach. (See the article and accompanying map on Massacre Bluff, page 58.)

The 1769 survey map on the next page shows a trailing sand bar in the river running parallel with our north peninsula. At low tide, this could certainly make navigation south more difficult. It also could collect fish. Farther south note "Orange Grove," which was planted during the First Spanish Period (1565-1763).

Probably Marques anchored in the channel near the current US Coast Guard Station in the "high sand dune" area around our present day Dune Circle.

The Indian method of trapping fish in weirs woven from palmetto fronds and reeds is shown in Le Moyne's accompanying sketch. Whether wading or from canoes, the Indians' preferred fishing technique was spearing fish with sharpened sticks or shell-tipped spears.

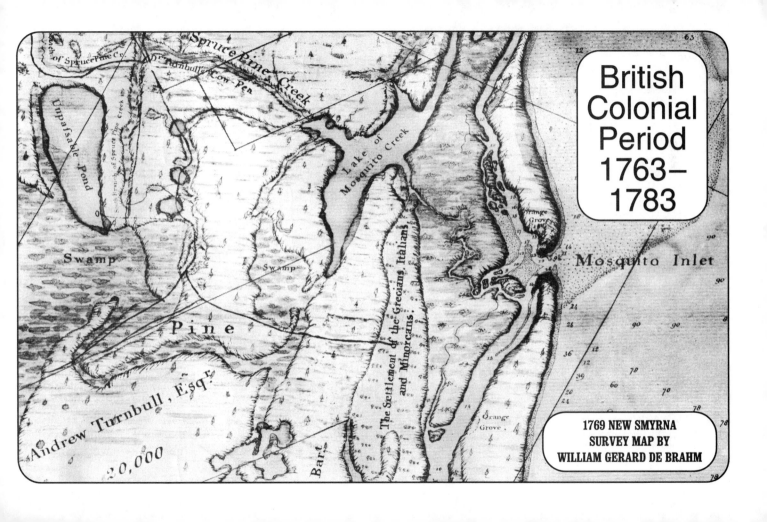

British
Colonial
Period
1763–
1783

1769 NEW SMYRNA
SURVEY MAP BY
WILLIAM GERARD DE BRAHM

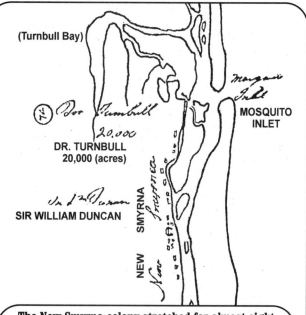

(Turnbull Bay)

MOSQUITO INLET

DR. TURNBULL
20,000 (acres)

SIR WILLIAM DUNCAN

NEW SMYRNA

The New Smyrna colony stretched for almost eight miles along the west bank of the river. This sketch (circa 1770) shows a string of buildings, the largest of which (a warehouse?) appears to be in the vicinity of the Old Stone Wharf. (Map courtesy of Dot Moore)

DR. ANDREW TURNBULL'S GREATEST VENTURE: THE NEW WORLD COLONY

Dr. Andrew Turnbull, a Scottish physician residing in London, followed a bold speculation. Mediterranean peoples already accustomed to warm climates would flourish in Britain's newly acquired Florida.

The original partnership was formed in 1766 between Turnbull and another doctor, Sir William Duncan, who was physician to King George III.

A third partner joined the venture: Lord George Grenville, former Prime Minister. However, Grenville used his kinsman, Sir Richard Temple, Commander of the Navy, to act on his behalf. Their agreement was signed April 2, 1767.

By June 1767 the three secured adjoining royal land grants of 20,000 acres each. Subsequent grants of 41,000 acres to Turnbull—21,400 for himself 5,000 acres for each of his four children—brought 101,400 acres under his control in East Florida.

Turnbull pledged he would provide personal on-site management; the other two partners would pay jointly no more than £9,000 over seven years. After seven years the partners would divide all the royal land grant property and proceeds into three equal parts, drawn by lot.

More doesn't always mean better. Originally, provisions had been made for 500 settlers, not the 1,255 who arrived. For the proprietors, more colonists meant more royal land grants could be made in the proportion of 100 acres for each head of household and 50 acres for additional family members.

For the colonists, the consequences of two-and-a-half times more people than provisions meant everything was in short supply. The colony was not self-sufficient; initially, it was scarcely a month away from starvation.

No wonder a rebellion broke out on August 19, 1768, shortly after all the colonists were settled at New Smyrna. The insurrection was quickly suppressed. Ringleaders were captured, tried and two were hung. (See "The 1768 New Smyrna Rebellion" on page 36.)

From its turbulent beginning, Turnbull's absentee shareholders had reason to be nervous. When the 1769 expenses far exceeded expectations, this agreement was renegotiated. In October Duncan and Temple agreed to add £24,000 to the venture if their share was increased to two-fifths each, with one fifth for Turnbull. Likewise, any new grants would be added to the company's property and divided into fifths.

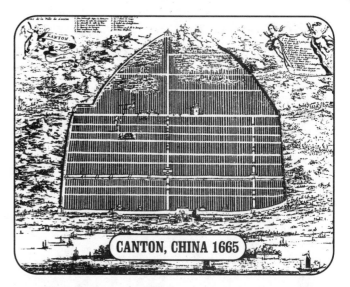

CANTON, CHINA 1665

"The nearness of the Hutts to one another gives the whole a Resemblance of an Eastern or Chinese plantation," Turnbull wrote to friend Lord Shelburne. By September 1769, almost 200 families were settled on farms along eight miles of the river. Each tract was 210 feet wide; their acreage reached westward.

Canton was one of the first Chinese cities to be visited by European travelers. Turnbull may have been alluding to this bird's-eye view map by Nieuhoff when he described the colony.

WAS THIS TURNBULL'S 300-ACRE AGRICULTURAL STATION?

Every time you've driven north past Art Center Avenue on US #1 toward the three bridges crossing Spruce Creek, you've passed through the first 300 acres of real estate that Dr. Andrew Turnbull acquired in New Smyrna.

Atlantic Center for the Arts is located on the southern portion of this 300-acre parcel fronting on Turnbull Bay. Turnbull's private plantation possibly was the first agricultural experiment station in the region.

"Mr. Turnbull has purchased Negroes, & forms a Cotton Plantation immediately, under the Direction of Skillful Planter, who he has prevailed with to settle upon his Estate; he had ordered a number of Cattle to be drove from Carolina and Georgia...to be put under the care of an Overseer, who has the management of a number of Artificers and Negroes, employed in clearing Ground and building Houses for the reception of Settlers," wrote Florida Governor James Grant on January 20, 1767.

The 1767 survey shows "Lagoon" (Turnbull Bay) and a small house labeled "Davis" at the northern tip. This the site is now occupied by a large frame house once owned by attorney Bob Matthews and later by Stetson University. It is south of the three bridges over Spruce Creek.

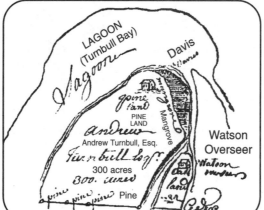

Continuing clockwise, another house with the notation "Watson, Overseer" is located to the east of US #1 where Murray Creek passes under the highway. Old US #1 ran through this settlement once known as "Sleepy Hollow" or Lourcey Point. "Pine" noted three times (bottom left) marks the southern boundary of the tract, in the vicinity of Art Center Avenue.

Evidence of a man-made shell causeway and sluice gates for rice cultivation, as well as indigo vats cut into the coquina ridge along Murray Creek can be found today just south of Cardinal Homes' development of "Creekside."

RIDE THE KING'S ROAD
NEW SMYRNA'S FIRST HIGHWAY

The Indians followed animal trails; the Spanish followed Indian trails; and the British followed portions of these original paths to create the first land route along Florida's East Coast. This "highway" began at the St. Mary's River, went to St. Augustine and south to New Smyrna.

Under the Treaty of Paris, Spain ceded Florida to the British in 1763 to recover the port of Havana. When Florida's first British Governor Col. James Grant arrived in 1764, over 3,000 Spanish had just been evacuated. Grant reported finding "a State of Nature, not an acre of land planted...and nobody to work or at work."

Roads were essential to British enterprise. Existing roads were narrow and in poor condition, even worse during rainy weather. Grant had no budget, so he raised subscriptions for the project. The road project from St. Augustine to New Smyrna was entrusted to Lt. Governor John Moultrie.

By December 1767 a passable road was "blazed by my (Indian) friend Grey Eyes when for three years others could not open one," Grant declared.

None too soon: the first four ships of New Smyrna colonists arrived at St. Augustine on June 26, 1768.

The King's Road was one a rough ride.

When all were gathered safely, some continued to New Smyrna by sea. Others, having suffered at sea long enough, chose to walk the final 70 miles to New Smyrna on the King's Road recently blazed by Grey Eyes.

"The 1,400 settlers...were sent, some by water and some by land to the Mosquettoes where all of them were fixed upon plantations," Grant informed London on August 10, 1768.

You can still follow of the King's Road, which includes portions of Mary Avenue to Enterprise Road, Pioneer Trail, Williams Road, and Letha Street. There a cedar bridge crossed Spruce Creek. Remains of a shell causeway on the north shore are visible west of the FEC Railway trestle. Today, the area is overgrown with marsh grass.

DR. ANDREW TURNBULL
BORN: February 12, 1720
Annan, Dumfresshire, Scotland
DIED: March 13, 1792

A graduate of Edinburgh University, Turnbull then studied medicine in Paris, France, where he met his wife, Gracia Maria Rubini.

MARRIED:
August 22, 1753
Smyrna, Greece
(today called Izmir, Turkey)

CHILDREN:
Jane, 1754
Nichol, 1756
Katherine, 1758
Maria Gracia, 1759
Jane, 1760
Margaret, 1761
Helen, 1763
Flora Gordon, 1766
William Duncan, 1770
Robert James, 1774
John, 1775
Frederick William, —

Five of the twelve children did not survive childhood. In 1792, Turnbull's will mentions seven children: Nichol, Mary, Jenny, Margaret, William Duncan, Robert James, and John.

See the family genealogical web site at:
http://osiris.pue.udlap.mx/turnbull/

GRACIA MARIA RUBINI
BORN: July 13, 1736
Smyrna, Greece
DIED: August 2, 1798

Educated in Paris, this great beauty also spoke German, which brought her to the attention of Queen Charlotte's court.

"OLD" SMYRNA: OUR BIBLICAL CONNECTION

"And unto the angel of the church of Smyrna, write: These things saith the first and the last, which was dead, and is alive; I know thy works, and tribulation, and poverty (but thou art rich), and I know the blasphemy of them which say they are Jews, and are not, but are the synagogue of Satan. Fear none of those things which thou shalt suffer: behold, the devil shall cast some of you into prison, and ye may be tried; and ye shall have tribulation ten days: be thou faithful unto death, and I will give thee a crown of life. He that hath an ear, let him hear what the Spirit saith unto the churches; He that overcometh shall not be hurt of the second death."

This quotation comes from The Bible, Book of Revelation, 2:8-11. "Old" Smyrna is located in western Turkey; it is called Izmir today.

New Smyrna was named in honor of Dr. Turnbull's wife, Gracia Maria Rubini, who was a resident of Smyrna. Our namesake was also a seaport, where orange groves flourished. It has been of historical importance in the Mediterranean for over 5,000 years.

Smyrna is the reputed birthplace of the Greek epic poet Homer (8th century B.C.). Homer was born by the banks of the Meles, a stream worshiped for its magical healing powers. He wrote his epic poems *The Iliad* and *The Odyssey* in a cave at the source of this stream.

Ancient Smyrna was renown for its architectural beauty: paved streets laid out in a rectilinear pattern. It was celebrated for its library, a school of medicine where Galen (the "Father of Medicine") studied, as well as thermal springs where Agamemnon stopped to treat his wounded soldiers. Smyrna was a favorite exile for condemned governors who had fallen out of favor with Rome. After Caesar's murder in 44 B.C., Brutus and Cassius convened their council of war here.

WE'RE NOT ALONE
According to *Johnson's Cyclopedia* (1884),
Home Knowledge Atlas (1889)
and *Hammond's Modern Atlas of the World* (1922):

Smyrna Landing, Delaware	Smyrna, Michigan
Smyrna, Georgia	Smyrna, New York
Smyrna, Iowa	Smryna, North Carolina
Smyrna, Indiana	Smryna, Ohio
Smyrna, Kentucky	Smyrna, South Carolina
Smyrna Mills, Maine	Smyrna, Tennessee

* New Smyrna is built on a high shelly bluff, on the West bank of the South branch of Musquito river, about ten miles above the capes of that river, which is about thirty miles North of Cape Canaveral, Lat. 28. I was there about ten years ago, when the surveyor run the lines or precincts of the colony, where there was neither habitation nor cleared field. It was then a famous orange grove, the upper or South promontory of a ridge, nearly half a mile wide, and stretching North about forty miles, to the head of the North branch of the Musquito, to where the Tomoko river unites with it, nearly parallel to the sea coast, and not above two miles across to the sea beach. All this ridge was then one entire orange grove, with live oaks, magnolias, palms, red bays, and others. I observed then, near where New Symrna now stands, a spacious Indian mount and avenue, which stood near the banks of the river : the avenue ran on a strait line back, through the groves, across the ridge, and terminated at the verge of natural savannas and ponds.

BEFORE TURNBULL'S COLONISTS ARRIVED: Naturalist William Bartram described the site of New Smyrna during its original survey in 1765-66. This facsimile reprint of a footnote is from the 1794 edition of *The Travels of William Bartram*.

NOTES ON BARTRAM'S TEXT

"South branch of Musquito river," First called Musquito River, Turnbull named it the Hillsborough River in honor of Wills Hill, First Earl of Hillsborough (1718-93), who was President of the Board of Trade and Secretary of State for the British Colonies. It was renamed Indian River North in 1901.

"I was there about ten years ago," It was 1765 when the first survey of the future site of New Smyrna was made by a team of surveyors headed by William Gerard de Brahm, Surveyor General to King George III.

"It was then a famous orange grove...nearly half a mile wide, and stretching North about forty miles..." Oranges are not native to Florida. They were introduced by the Spanish during their first 200-year occupation. Oranges traveled from China, to India, to Italy, to Spain.

Before the British gained possession of Florida in 1763, an area of 24 Spanish leagues called "St. Ana de Afafa" belonged to the heirs of Don Joachin de Florencia. This huge grant stretched from Spruce Creek south for 15.78 miles and west for 10.52 miles (one Spanish land league equals 2.63 miles).

"Orange grove" is meant as a concentration of trees, not necessarily the neat rows we might imagine. The trees were interspersed as Bartram describes with "live oaks, magnolias, palms, red bays, and others."

"Near where New Smyrna now stands," By Turnbull's own description, New Smyrna stretched for almost eight miles along the west bank of the river. No doubt, the heart of this agricultural colony's import and export activities was centered near the Old Stone Wharf at Clinch Street and South Riverside Drive.

"A spacious Indian mount and avenue" Half a mile north of the Old Stone Wharf is the Old Fort Park mound. Whether its curious coquina foundation was concealed by this large Indian shell mound or whether it was built after Bartram's visit is not definitely known.

The "avenue ran on a strait line back," probably followed the course of Canal Street. The "natural savannas and ponds" are still visible near the New Smyrna Beach Regional Shopping Center on SR 44.

Compare this text to Bartram's description of Mt. Royal on the St. Johns River: "a noble Indian highway, which led from the great mount, on a strait line" and ended "on the verge of an oblong artificial lake" on the "edge of an extensive green level savanna. The grand highway was about fifty yards wide...earth thrown up on each side, making a bank about two feet high."

SPAIN AND PORTUGAL
Scale, 1:3,500,000
English Miles

Boundaries of Provinces (Spain) and Districts (Portugal).
Capitals of Provinces and Districts
Districts in Portugal have the same name as the Capital town
Boundaries of former Provinces
Railways — Canals Passes Fortifications
Co. = Cerro; P.; = Pico, Mountain peak; Pto. = Puerto, Pass;
Sa. = Serra, Sierra, Mountains Swamps

Who are the Minorcans? Here's a view of their home in the Balearic Islands, east of Spain in the Mediterranean Sea. They comprised over two-thirds of the New Smyrna colony.

Mahón is the port city of Minorca, which is also the origin of that popular salad dressing we call "mayonnaise." It is appropriately named for the city's people—the Mahónese.

This port also served as the staging area for all the colonists Turnbull had gathered to join his New World colony. Italians, 110 men, were recruited from Leghorn (Livorno), a port city in Tuscany. They were sent to Mahón to await his Greek recruits. While they waited for Turnbull's return, *amore* happened. Most of the Italian bachelors took Minorcan wives. The Greeks came from Corsica and the village of Mani on the Greek Peloponnesus; others came from the Aegean islands and from Greek settlements in Turkey.

Accounts from different authors vary, but the 1,403 colonists who began the journey included approximately 100-200 Italians, 200 Greeks, 50 Corsican-Greeks, 6 French, 5 Majorcans, 2 Catalans, and 1,000 Minorcans. Only 1,255 actually arrived at the New Smyrna colony by August 1768.

American Soldier 145
Betsy 120
Charming Betsy 232
Elizabeth 190
Friendship 198
Henry and Carolina 142
Hope 150
New Fortune 226

TOTAL: 1,403
MEN, WOMEN AND CHILDREN

Fearing Barbary pirates, Turnbull's fleet was escorted through Gibraltar to the Madeira Islands by the British frigate *Carysford*. The three-month journey to Florida took its toll: 28 died on one ship. Of the 1,403 original settlers recruited, only 1,255 set foot in the New World.

Pirate alert! Turnbull's colonists didn't set off on some pleasure boat cruise. This 1860's steel engraving, "Pirates of the Mediterranean Playing at Dice for Prisoners," suggests yet another reason for concern by the intrepid voyagers.

Four Barbary States in North Africa—Morocco, Algiers, Tunis, and Tripoli—had prospered from piracy for centuries. Even the young United States agreed to pay $18,000 for piracy protection in 1799. When the price went up in 1801, the US Navy was dispatched to blockade "the shores of Tripoli."

"Millions for defense, but not one cent for tribute" was the battle cry. The Marines stormed the fort at Tripoli in 1805, which is commemorated in the Marine Corps invocation hymn.

Any good contract should seek to avoid misunderstandings by specifying the terms of agreement. However, if you were a New Smyrna colonist, the terms of your indenture probably weren't clear, especially concerning length of service and the amount of land offered. The future seeds of discontent were planted in this fertile confusion.

Basically, the three-month voyage to Florida was "free." You were promised good victuals and clothing. If you didn't like Florida you would be allowed to return home at their own expense. There is no record of anyone returning to their Mediterranean homeland.

If you stayed and worked for 3, 5, 7, 8 or 10 years (accounts vary), you would be granted 50 acres for every head of household plus 5 (or 25) acres for each child.

The sole copy this contract was found in Mahón, Minorca, written in Spanish and signed only by Turnbull.

It states clearly: "Mr. Turnbull, within the period of ten years, can neither discharge nor take from his service any of the below signed contractors, and equally none of them can separate from his service before having completed the ten years." After the fall of the colony in 1777, Turnbull and his family moved to Charleston, SC. Years later, Turnbull's own description of land ownership by colonists included mention of a 99-year lease.

Author, surveyor's draftsman and Turnbull critic Bernard Romans wrote the settlers were to receive "a pitiful portion of land for ten years, upon the plan of the feudal system: this being improved and just rendered fit for cultivation, at the end of that term it again reverts to the original grantor, and the grantee, may, if he chooses, begin a new cycle of vassalage for ten years more."

During their St. Augustine depositions in 1777, none of the colonists mention any document was signed prior to their indenture. They all refer to an "agreement."

A three-year famine caused Turnbull's recruitment of Minorcans to be overly successful, resulting over twice as many colonists as anticipated—including almost 200 stowaways. Of course, oral agreements were easier and quicker than obtaining properly signed documents. Since many of the colonists could neither read nor write, the probability of misunderstanding was guaranteed.

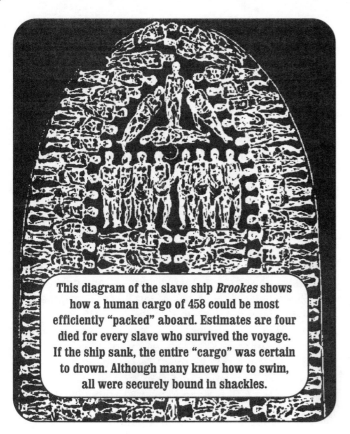

This diagram of the slave ship *Brookes* shows how a human cargo of 458 could be most efficiently "packed" aboard. Estimates are four died for every slave who survived the voyage. If the ship sank, the entire "cargo" was certain to drown. Although many knew how to swim, all were securely bound in shackles.

DID 500 SLAVES BOUND FOR NEW SMYRNA PERISH?

Did 500 African slaves drown en route to the New Smyrna colony? Johann David Schoepf (1752-1800) was the original source for this account which appears in his *Travels in the Confederation: 1783-1784.*

After the fall of the New Smyrna colony in 1777, Dr. Andrew Turnbull and his family "retired in disgust to Charleston [South Carolina], where I made his acquaintance," Shoepf explained.

Turnbull's colony was an agricultural enterprise. The soil was rich, but required land clearing, as well as digging miles of canals for drainage and irrigation.

"But the delicate Greeks were no ways pleased with the unavoidable hardships of subduing wild land. To be sure, for making the work easier the company had provided for negroes who were to be hired out among the Greeks; but unluckily the first ship, bringing 500 negroes from Africa, was wrecked on the coast of Florida and the whole number was lost."

In 1921, Henry H. Read's *The Waterways of Florida* added that this slave ship from Jamaica "was driven by a storm off the Bahama Banks and all hands were lost."

This quaint coquina bridge built in the early 1900's was located east of the Chamber of Commerce, 115 Canal Street. (Photo by F.C. Van de Sande)

HOW DID "CANAL" STREET GET ITS OBVIOUS NAME?

Canal Street was named for an extensive system of canals dug beginning in 1768. This main canal—the Turnbull Canal—was covered by the north sidewalk along Canal Street in 1924.

Today the main canal surfaces at Myrtle Avenue, running parallel to West Canal Street...although you might suspect it was just another ditch. In the public park across the street, a smaller canal runs north-south, parallel to Myrtle Avenue down to 10th Street.

Agriculture would be the life blood of the New Smyrna colony. During his travels throughout the Mediterranean, New Smyrna's founder Dr. Andrew Turnbull had seen Egyptian irrigation methods on the Nile River delta. He was one of the first to introduce "the Egyptian's mode of watering" to the New World.

Irrigation and drainage of the rich swamp lands resulted in nearly 3,000 acres of improved land claimed at New Smyrna during the 1770's. Its success was apparent. In the first year, 5,000 bushels of corn were exported. By 1772, the export of indigo provided Turnbull and his partners £3,000.

The colonists brought cuttings of grapes, olives and mulberries (to feed silkworms) from their Mediterranean homes. Corn, cotton, figs, hemp, indigo, rice, and sugar were planted.

Cochineal insects were introduced for making scarlet dye; their white cocoons can still be seen on prickly pear cacti throughout the area. Glasswort (also called "chicken fingers") was collected from the marshes and burned to make barilla, an impure form of sodium carbonate used in soap and glass manufacture.

Although the colonists were not familiar with the cultivation of hemp, cotton or indigo, these were crops on which the British crown had placed a bounty.

Since the land was "well adapted to the Growth of Hemp or Flax it shall be a Condition of the Grant...the Grantee shall sow and continue Annually to Cultivate a due proportion of the Land not less than one acre in every thousand, with that beneficial Article of Produce." Its purpose was to supply the British navy with canvas and rope. With 101,400 acres under Turnbull's supervision, the grant required 101 acres planted in hemp.

Today, hemp (*cannabis sativa*) would be recognized as marijuana. For 5,000 years its original use was rope, twine, oakum, canvas, paper, hempseed oil, and as a drug that was listed in the *National Formulary* until 1937.

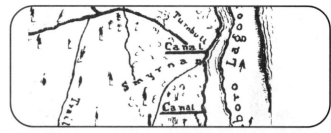

1839 military map shows the Canal Street (top) canal and the South (Gabordy) Canal, now the city limits between New Smyrna Beach and Edgewater. The King's Road shows at top center.

The South or Gabordy Canal looking east toward the South Riverside Drive bridge. Oral tradition claims the Turnbull colony's men dug the Canal Street canal while the women widened an existing creek to create the South Canal.

THE 1768 NEW SMYRNA REBELLION

In some beginnings the end is foretold. The Turnbull colonists' three-month voyage from the Mediterranean took its toll—28 died in one ship alone. Although 1,403 set out, only 1,255 arrived in New Smyrna. Little did they know when they landed in Florida that by year's end 300 adults and 150 children would be dead.

After arriving in St. Augustine, some of the colonists marched down the King's Road to New Smyrna. The rest arrived by sea. Because the colony had been stocked for 500 settlers, everything was in short supply. Communal huts and kitchens were established. Food was scarce; the cook was accused of stealing food. Although the waters were filled with fish, the colonists were forbidden to spend time away from the fields. A cargo of 500 slaves bound for New Smyrna wrecked along the Florida coast. All the slaves aboard were lost. The hard work of clearing fields and digging irrigation and drainage canals fell to the settlers.

At least four different languages were spoken in the colony—a veritable Tower of Babel story. Some of the English overseers were used to working slaves and treated the colonists as such. Instead of the luxury and quietude of sleep, there were swarms of mosquitoes. This certainly wasn't the Eden promised by Turnbull.

Rebellion broke out two weeks after the last colonist arrived in New Smyrna. Turnbull had left for St. Augustine, spending the night at Mt. Oswald, a sugar plantation on the Halifax River near today's Ormond Beach.

At 11 o'clock on August 19, 1768, the colonists abandoned their work and gathered in the center of town. They were angry, trapped and desperate. The plan was to flee the colony for the safety of Havana.

A supply ship had just arrived from St. Augustine; it was immediately captured. Carlo Forni, an Italian overseer, declared himself "Captain General and

Commander in Chief." In the excitement, store houses were broken into—blankets, linen, fishing tackle, flour, firearms, and ammunition were loaded aboard the commandeered ship. A cow was killed (then a British capital offense) for meat during their voyage. Rum and oil barrels that couldn't be loaded were staved in the streets. Clear thinking and planning ceased when a barrel of rum was opened and consumed.

The mutineers included nearly all the Greeks and Italians in the colony. The Minorcans, to a man, refused to join in the rioting. Although Forni threatened death to anyone who attempted to warn authorities, two Italians "faithful to their master" slipped into the swamps at dusk and headed for Turnbull's plantation, four miles north of New Smyrna. Turnbull was visiting friends at Mt. Oswald.

An overseer in charge sent a rider to Mt. Oswald to inform Turnbull. At midnight Turnbull received the news, drafted a hasty letter to Governor Grant in St. Augustine, and in the early hours of August 20th another express rider was racing toward St. Augustine.

At New Smyrna, Guiseppe Massiadoli and his knife mutilated one of the most hated overseers, an Englishman named Cutter. There are three accounts: 1) Cutter had his ears and nose cut off; 2) an ear and two fingers were removed; and 3) lost his right ear and three fingers from his right hand, then was stabbed in the groin. Afterwards, the delirious Cutter was locked in a storeroom.

Turnbull returned to New Smyrna the morning of August 20th and rescued his wounded overseer. Cutter's continued bleeding had left him in serious condition, raving about his assailants. He eventually died.

The colony was in chaos. About 300 mutineers were on board. They hadn't finished loading the ship because they had been feasting and drinking most of the night. The plan was to sail on the 11 a.m. tide on the 22nd.

Governor Grant received Turnbull's plea for help; he dispatched the provincial frigate *East Florida* and another vessel under sail "with Troops, Provisions, Ammunition and everything necessary to pursue the Greeks." Another detachment under Major Whitmore marched down the King's Road to New Smyrna.

The *East Florida* found the mutineers' vessel at the Inlet, waiting to sail with the 11 o'clock tide. One cannon volley was enough to persuade them to surrender. However, during the commotion 35 mutineers jumped into a smaller boat and headed south.

In turn, they were pursued by the smaller vessel accompanying the *East Florida*. Several weeks later the renegades were captured in the Florida Keys, barely 100 miles from their destination, Havana, Cuba.

Governor Grant's next problem was what to do with 20 rebels he now held in prison. Of five, he had no doubt: "The proof against them is said to be clear. In that case they probably [will] be made Examples of."

The trial was held January 1769. Three were sentenced to death: Carlo Forni, for piracy; Guiseppe Massiadoli, for cutting off two fingers and an ear of the overseer, Cutter; and Elia Medici, for killing the cow— then a capital offense.

Medici was given an extraordinary difficult choice: his life would be spared if he would execute the other two. A Dutch surveyor and author, Bernard Romans, was a member of the jury and witnessed the execution.

"On this occasion I saw one of the most moving scenes I ever experienced; long and obstinate was the struggle of this man's mind, who repeatedly called out, that he chose to die rather than to be executioner of his friends in distress; this not a little perplexed Mr. Woodridge, the sheriff, till at last the entreaties of the victims themselves, put an end to to the conflict in his breast, by encouraging him to act.

"Now we beheld a man thus compelled to mount the ladder, take leave of his friends in the most moving manner, kissing them the moment before he committed them to an ignominious death," Romans reported in his book *A Concise History of East and West Florida.*

Because manpower was precious and an example had been made, a full pardon was granted to the other ringleaders: Georgi Stephanopoli, for commandeering the supply vessel which belonged to Sir Charles Burdett; and Clatha Corona, for breaking into the warehouse.

Initially, Turnbull estimated losses suffered £400-500 "at most." He later placed a value of £2,000 on the items loaded on the commandeered vessel, of which £1,300 worth was thrown into the water when the rebels found the schooner too heavy to clear the Inlet.

After the rebellion, Governor Grant proposed construction of a fort. The project was begun, but never finished. A guard of a sergeant and eight men was stationed at New Smyrna until 1777, when political intrigues, cancellation of of indentures, and the stirrings of the American Revolution led to the fall of the colony.

In May 1777 the courts in St. Augustine heard shocking depositions of abuse from the New Smyrna colonists. Most were released from their indentures. Within a month about 600 deserted New Smyrna and marched en masse 60 miles up the King's Road to St. Augustine. The largest British colony in the New World had resolutely walked away.

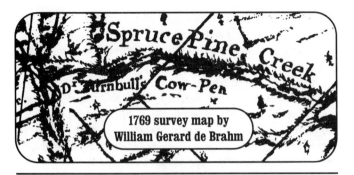

1769 survey map by
William Gerard de Brahm

INDIAN SHOWDOWN AT TURNBULL'S COW-PEN

The New Smyrna colonists' fear of Indians began with the birth of the colony. Particularly, the Indians hated the Spanish. Governor of Florida James Grant assured the Indians repeatedly that the Minorcan settlers were not Spanish—even if they looked similar and spoke the same language. This explanation sufficed two years.

In May 1771 the Upper Creek Indian Chief Cowkeeper, Chief Long Warrior, an unnamed third head man, and 72 braves arrived in New Smyrna. They had heard rumors the colony included Spaniards and the equally hated Yemasee Indians.

The Indians severely beat a Minorcan boat crew on Spruce Pine Creek (Spruce Creek) near Dr. Turnbull's Cow-Pen shown on the accompanying 1769 survey map. The Cow-Pen was near Letha Street (formerly Robinson Road), west of the FEC Railway trestle.

Alarm spread throughout the colony; Turnbull, who was in St. Augustine, was summoned home. He invited the head men and 20 braves into his house, treating them generously with food and drink. Describing the incident later, Turnbull praised Chief Cowkeeper as "A Sober manly Indian...very watchful over the others for fear they should do anything wrong."

Some of the braves got drunk, but Cowkeeper had them beaten "very severely" when they suggested killing a calf in Turnbull's Cow-Pen.

After a two-day visit with Turnbull, the Indians broke camp. One party returned home to the St. Johns River. The other group was escorted to the southern limits of the plantations by Turnbull's overseer Langley Bryant and a slave, Black Sandy. The Indians sought proof of Turnbull's claim that no Yemasee were in the area. They found none and were satisfied.

A few days later Chief Long Warrior asked Turnbull for one calf for his hungry people. Turnbull promptly obliged; the Indians left peaceably.

THE FALL OF NEW SMYRNA FOLLOWS SHOCKING DEPOSITIONS
St. Augustine, May 7–20, 1777

"HOW LONG MUST I SERVE YOU?"

Anthony Stephanopoli asked, "Good sir, let me know how long I must serve you?" Usually unspoken, it was a common question in the colony. Stephanopoli had served Dr. Turnbull for nine years and four months, although he originally had agreed to serve only six years.

Turnbull promised to pay five pounds sterling per year: one half to be paid at the end of the year, the other half to be paid after six years. Stephanopoli testified he never received a farthing.

Furthermore, he was promised two pounds of fresh bread a day, or if no bread, then 18 to 20 ounces of biscuit; and one pound of fresh meat per day, or if no fresh meat was available, one-half pound of salt pork. Also one pint of wine per day, or if no wine was available, a pint of whatever liquor was to be had. It didn't happen.

Stephanopoli participated in the August 1768 rebellion. After the rebellion, people continued to starve and began to die, 10 or 11 a day...some days 15.

He ran away; it would be better to die in the woods than to endure this miserable condition. He was pursued, caught and received 110 lashes on his bare back. Then a 15-pound chain was attached to his leg.

His sustenance was five quarts of hominy grits a week, except for a half pint of rice for Sunday dinner.

He was obliged to work in the fields with the chain on his leg. After work, he was locked up in a room every night. He did not receive clothes for two years and had one blanket during the entire nine-year ordeal.

BEGS FOR BREAD FROM HIS SICK BED

Nichola Delmache's cousin Peter was driven from his sick bed back to work and beaten with a stick by Nichola Moveritte, one of Turnbull's overseers.

During another sickness, Moveritte entered his room and ordered him to go back to work. If he could not work, Demalache was told to lie down near the communal kitchen. He was to be given no victuals. After everyone had their supper, Peter Demalache begged "for God's sake" a little broth from his sick bed near the kitchen.

No one answered his call. The next morning when the colonists went back to the fields, they found Peter where they had left him. He was dead; his body was "covered with mosquitoes all full of blood."

TIED TO A TREE AND WHIPPED

Pompey Possey said Dr. Turnbull beat him on horseback, dismounted and beat him again, striking him in his private parts. He was obliged to "lay in a palmetto house in the field all night, not being able to go home."

Pompey was also accused of knowing about a runaway. Although he denied it, he was taken to the guard house and put in irons for three or four days. Then he was removed, tied to a tree and given 35 lashes.

After his pleurisy had lingered for two months, he missed one day of work. When he returned the next day, Turnbull "broke two sticks about him, as big as his thumb, and took him by the hair and beat him with his fist in his breast, 'till he was tired, and then dragged him through the field."

FLOGGING WAS A DAILY OCCURRENCE

Juan Portella agreed to serve Turnbull for five years as a shoemaker. Instead, he was sent to the field and never worked at his trade.

Since he was not used to farming, he was slow at the task. Too bad. As punishment, overseer Nichola Moveritte put him on half allowance and sometimes none. Portella claimed he was flogged almost every day because he could not work as well as the rest.

TEN-YEAR-OLD BEATEN, THEN STONED

Michael Alamon testified that a ten-year-old boy Biel Venis was very sick in his room. Overseer Lewis Pouchintena arrived, beat the boy and drove him out to work in the field. The boy was not able to work.

Pouchinetena put him on a stump in the field and ordered the rest of the boys to pelt Venis with stones. The youngster died on the spot.

RUNAWAY GETS 113 LASHES AND LEG CHAIN

Goisefa Marcatto was "badly used and almost starved to death, working days and nights, not even Sunday excepted." Seven quarts of hominy grits and eight ounces of pork per week were allowed him.

Starvation was prevalent; he joined some others trying to run away. They were caught; he was brought back and confined in jail. A 24-pound chain was attached to his leg when he was released. Next he was tied to a tree and received 113 lashes. For six months he was worked with the chain on his leg; a sentry accompanied him. At night he was placed in jail, chained to a log.

After six years, he asked Turnbull to be discharged. He was placed in the stocks, night and day. For fear of being chained by the leg and starved, Marcatto signed a paper to serve Turnbull for four more years.

EVEN THE BLACKSMITH RECEIVES 50 LASHES

Louis Margau worked as a blacksmith in the colony. Like the others, any good victuals and wages promised were never received. After he had served out his indenture, he asked Turnbull for his discharge.

Turnbull asked Margau to follow him. They entered the jail where he received 50 lashes and was confined with little food other than a little Indian corn and water.

Turnbull also reassigned his wife's duties, separating her from her six-month-old infant. She was allowed to visit the child twice a day to nurse the infant.

After two weeks, Margau "seeing the miserable condition of his wife and child, and likewise himself was in, being almost starved, he was forced to sign a paper to serve Dr. Turnbull five years longer...."

OVERSEER SIMON'S DEADLY ABUSE EXPOSED

Giosefa Lurance had already been disabled by Simon, one of the overseers. Sadly, there were several other incidents involving his family members.

This same overseer asked his sister-in-law Paola if she would sleep with him. She refused. A few days later, Paola was at her work and Simon immediately found fault with her progress and began to beat her with a stick.

"For God's sake, corporal, don't beat me, for I am big with child and you will kill my child," Paola pleaded.

"I don't care for you nor your child. I don't care if you both go to hell," Simon answered.

About three days later she delivered a dead baby.

Finally, his brother Matthew was taken sick with a bellyache. Simon came into the field and found him leaning over a stump. A bellyache wasn't a good reason.

"You lie; you are lazy," Simon yelled and began to beat him "with a large stick 'till it wore out, and then beat the said Matthew Lurance with his fist 'till he was tired, and then stamped on him with his feet for a long time."

Later, Simon gave him another beating and left him in the field. Matthew eventually found his way home.

He "lay in his bed for about three months, with the blood running down his back, and then he died...some short time before his death he told the people that he was dying, but that it was not God almighty that killed him. It was Simon."

POSTSCRIPT: NEW SMYRNA COLONY FAILS

Twenty-one depositions were given by 17 individuals during May 7–20, 1777. Six deponents were Minorcan colonists; 11 were the Greek or Italian. Their indentures were revoked. Within a month, 600 deserted New Smyrna and settled in St. Augustine.

SECOND
SPANISH
PERIOD
1783-1821

Steel engraving from *Picturesque America*, 1872.   Edited by William Cullen Bryant.

The Rock House stood on an Indian shell mound and commanded an excellent view of our inlet. Was it an ancient lookout? The entire site was destroyed when the FEC Railway excavated the shell underneath for road bed fill.

THE CURIOUS HISTORY OF THE ROCK HOUSE

Was it by chance the Rock House stood opposite Ponce de Leon Inlet, built on a high Indian shell mound? It commanded an excellent view of any naval activity. Today, on the east side of US #1 across from the New Smyrna Municipal Airport, you'll find a depression where the shell mound and Rock House once stood.

The FEC Railway acquired the site in 1901 and built a railroad spur to the Rock House. The two-story coquina structure was destroyed when shell was excavated for road bed fill and carried away on railroad cars. By 1907 all evidence of the site had disappeared.

Unfortunately, the shell was so ancient that it crumbled and proved to be unsuitable fill. Many celts, arrowheads, bone implements, and plummets were recovered from the mound at that time.

The earliest recorded occupation of this site was an 1803 Spanish land grant of 400 acres made to Henry Martin. He continued in possession until 1808 when the house was burned and his plantation destroyed by Indians. Since the Spanish offered no protection, he was forced to abandon his holding. Later, his father-in-law occupied the property "with uncommon patience and suffering" until 1812. He left a tenant living in the Rock House in 1821. This was the last inhabited house south of St. Augustine at that time.

In 1887 John Detwiler, the first editor of the *New Smyrna Breeze* newspaper, discovered a stone platform just north of the Rock House. He supposed it was a gun traverse, describing a "circular mound about four-feet high and approximately 12 or more feet across, with an opening in the center just 12 inches square. This contained the remains of a stick of live oak, evidently built in the masonry, but then decomposed until only a piece six-feet long flattened diagonally, with a large tenon or pivot on the upper end remained."

Later, Detwiler discovered Bertola Pacetti, who lived near the lighthouse, had "removed the circular stones for the purpose of building a cistern and found that the structure was a low circular tower with a stone platform around it and a post in the center."

Other accounts indicate the Rock House was approximately 20 x 36 feet. It contained a huge fireplace with niches located in the walls near the fireplace, evidently intended for images of Romanist worship. The floor was tabby, a "cement" made from shell mortar. The walls were about a foot thick.

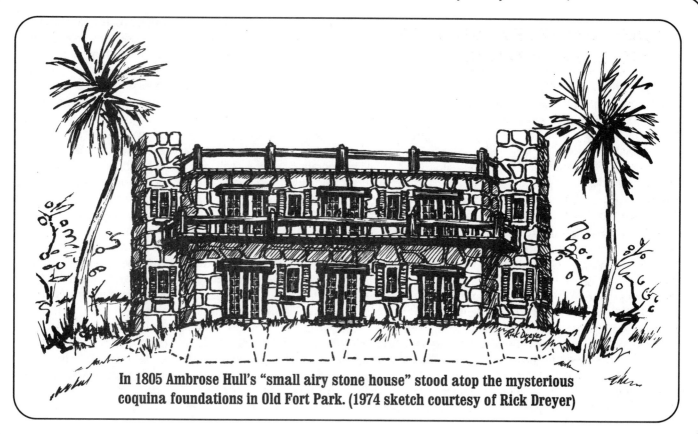

In 1805 Ambrose Hull's "small airy stone house" stood atop the mysterious coquina foundations in Old Fort Park. (1974 sketch courtesy of Rick Dreyer)

1805: TWO-STORY HOUSE ATOP THE OLD FORT FOUNDATIONS

From 500 B.C., a large Indian shell mound evolved at Washington Street and North Riverside Drive. It was noted as the Indian village "Caparaca" on Captain Alvaro Mexia's 1605 reconnaissance map.

Built into this mound was a substantial 55' x 86' coquina foundation, boasting walls five-and-a-half-feet thick. Some claim it was a Spanish fort, predating St. Augustine; others believe this was Turnbull's town mansion, although it wasn't built on his 20,000-acre royal land grant.

According to the Turnbull Palace theory, work was never completed before the fall of the colony in 1777 when the colonists marched en masse to St. Augustine. Thereafter, Turnbull and his family moved to Charleston, SC.

Ambrose Hull clearly describes "a wing—turret or tower" on each end of his two-story stone house built in 1805. However, he probably added this feature to an existing structure–that curious coquina foundation we know as the "Old Fort."

During the Second Spanish Period (1783-1821), Dr. Ambrose Hull, an Episcopal minister from Wallingford, Connecticut, answered Spain's call for colonists in Florida. Hull was granted 2,600 acres at New Smyrna in 1801. He established a cotton and sugar plantation.

Hull had "a number of masons employed in building a small airy stone house of two stories," he wrote to his brother-in-law on June 12, 1805.

On June 27 he further described their new house called Olive Mount to his sister-in-law: "Our house is built of hewn stone two stories—In the main body of the house are two large rooms one above the other—three double doors and six windows in each—at each end is a wing—turret or tower—in each two handsome bedrooms with three windows. The roofs are flat & terraced on which I spend some hours every fair day in walking & reading—and from which we have a charming prospect of the bar & Ocean...."

Hull's "wing—turret or tower" are located on the north and south ends, jutting out about four feet from the original foundation. This airy "sleeping room" feature was clearly added to an existing foundation. It is curious Hull would describe so modestly a house with over 9,400 sq. ft. as a "small airy stone house of two stories."

Hull died in 1821. In 1834, his heirs claimed over $12,500 in damages to his New Smyrna holdings, which were destroyed during the Patriot's War of 1812.

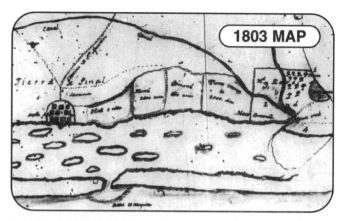

1803 MAP

45 acres of Sea-Island Cotton planting and growing, equal to
   5625 lbs. or 16 bales containing each 351 lbs. @ $60 .... 3357.00
20 acres of common cotton, equal to 200 bushels @ $2.00 ..... 400.00
2 acres of Sweet Potatoes, equal to 500 bushels @ $.25 .... 125.00
Garden Vegetables equal to say 50.00
4 horses at $50 each 200.00
Stock of provisions on hand left by Hull in his flight,
   (corn, poatoes, flour, etc.) 250.00
40 Bales of Short Staple Cotton on hand,
   14,000 pounds @ $.31 .... 4340.00
4 Hogsheads of Jamaica Rum,
   say 120 gallons each @ $1.25 per gallon 600.00
Large Stone dwelling house nearly destroyed,
   damage at a reasonable calculation 2000.00
Negro houses destroyed, reasonable amount of damage 500.00
Quantity of valuable furniture left in house, lost or destroyed ... 700.00
                                                      TOTAL $12534.00

Ambrose Hull began his cotton and sugar plantation in 1801. An early Indian attack caused a $3,000 loss. Starting anew, several settlers from New Providence, Bahama Islands, asked permission to join him, providing mutual protection from Indian attacks. Hull agreed and the joint settlement began in September 1803 until 1809 when the Bahamian settlers left.

This crude map shows the 1803 land grants. The center of town is a dome-shaped clearing in the forest at the Old Stone Wharf. It appears 11 buildings are clustered together.

Moving north (right) are the grants of Ambrose Hull, James Munroe, James Ormond, vacant land, and Robert McHardy on both sides of Spruce Creek.

LEFT: A helicopter view of the Old Fort Park ruins reveals the magnitude of our downtown history mystery. The lime mortar used (called tabby) was produced by burning oyster shells.

North Riverside Drive is to the right; the Municipal Yacht Basin is beyond. This photo was taken by the author in 1974. Note the chimney at the top right (northeast) corner of the ruins has since been destroyed by vandals.

RIGHT: Looking from the southeast corner of the ruins, the east wall is 86 feet and the west wall is 87 feet. Its width is a consistent 55 feet. Exterior walls are 5.5 feet thick, excluding the buttresses. The interior walls vary, averaging 4.5 feet. The buttresses rise at all exterior corners and foundation wall intersections. None of the buttresses exhibit the same profile.

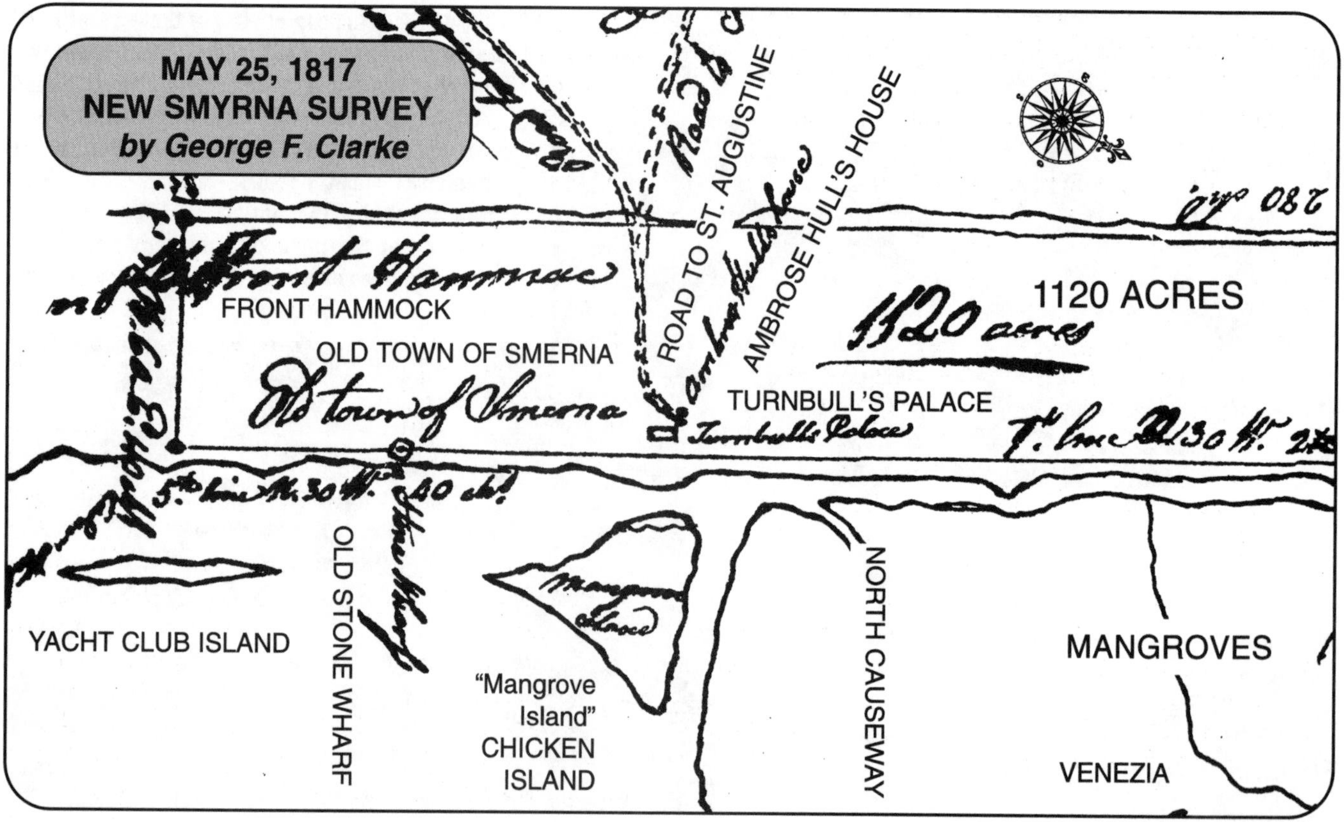

MAY 25, 1817
NEW SMYRNA SURVEY
by George F. Clarke

FRONT HAMMOCK

OLD TOWN OF SMERNA

ROAD TO ST. AUGUSTINE

AMBROSE HULL'S HOUSE

1120 ACRES

TURNBULL'S PALACE

YACHT CLUB ISLAND

OLD STONE WHARF

"Mangrove Island"
CHICKEN ISLAND

NORTH CAUSEWAY

MANGROVES

VENEZIA

NOTES ON CLARKE'S 1817 SURVEY

Yacht Club Island (South Island) began as just another sand bar. In February 1970 the city sold the north end of the island to developer John Gross for $65,000.

Old Stone Wharf was one of the Turnbull colonists' first public works. Judging by its present disarray, many coquina blocks have been "borrowed," possibly used by some of the houses along South Riverside Drive.

Old Town of Smerna identifies the original "center" of town near the Old Stone Wharf, both in Turnbull's time (1768-77) and during the following settlement of Ambrose Hull (1801-12). The southern boundary of this survey is one-half mile south of the wharf, about 5th Street and Commodore Drive on Yacht Club Island.

Chicken Island was sand bar, also shown on a 1769 survey map (see page 21). Here pioneer vegetation such as mangrove began to flourish. In more recent history, the droppings from too many roosting birds have killed these mangroves, as well as other islands in the Indian River North.

Road to St. Augustine follows the course of the King's Road including portions of Mary Avenue, Enterprise and Pioneer Trail. The other branch ran southwest to the "Cedar Bridge" at the intersection of today's Josephine Street and Old Mission Road.

Turnbull's Palace is the location of the massive Old Fort Park foundation. Curiously, the "palace" wasn't built on Dr. Andrew Turnbull's 20,000-acre grant, but rather on that of his partner, Sir William Duncan.

Over-designed and over-built, this foundation is more substantial than most modern construction. In 1996 mortar was discovered on the bottom course of the foundation blocks in the northwest corner. This suggests a floor. To keep something in or out? Were the nine separate compartments used for food storage?

Or could name "palace" be meant in an ironic sense, if this structure had actually been used as a prison to punish the Turnbull colonists?

Ambrose Hull's House is shown nearby, northwest of the Old Fort foundation, five years after the Hulls left New Smyrna. Yet his description of the house in 1805 indicates it had "a wing—turret or tower," exactly as those found on the Old Fort foundation. Hull's own correspondence suggests the building was completed in six weeks. Did he build on a previous foundation? In 1834, Hull's "small airy stone house of two stories" was claimed by his heirs as "a large stone building" valued at $2,000 that was destroyed during the 1812 Patriot's War.

If your real estate had been swapped around from Spanish to British, Spanish to US Territory, and finally had attained statehood, you'd be worn out, too.

Florida was one of the first six states to secede, joining the Confederacy in January 1861. After four years of war, the South surrendered. However, the strict terms for rejoining the Union included a divisive plan called Reconstruction (1865-77).

Small wonder the state motto in the early 1870's reflected a new, belligerent tone: LET US ALONE. It was a warning, but no one seemed to listen. Hunters and sports fishermen came first. Then the railroads arrived in the 1890's with thousands of winter visitors.

Thereafter, "We skin gators in the summer and tourists in the winter" became the new motto, old timers joked.

LET US ALONE

FLORIDA.

FLORIDA TERRITORIAL PERIOD
1821–1845

FLORIDA STATEHOOD – September 1845

YOU'RE IN THE ARMY NOW: FORT NEW SMYRNA, 1839

The Second Seminole War (1835-42) was the longest war in our history until Vietnam. When Spain ceded Florida to the United States for $5,000,000 in 1821, the United States promised to recognize the rights of all Spanish subjects.

Unfortnately, the United States forgot Spain had officially accorded that status to the Indians as well. An 1830 edict ordered all Indians deported from their homelands to west of the Mississippi River. Not surprisingly, the Indians rebelled in 1835.

The prevailing national attitude toward Indians became evident soon after the Revolutionary War. The *United States Magazine* (circa 1780) boldly proclaimed:

"The whole earth given to man and all the children of Adam have an equal right to it and equal parts of it...the revealed law has given earth to man under fixed conditions that he use it in the sweat of his brow.

"Now Indians do not use their extensive woods in the sweat of their brow but only hunt there. Therefore it is plain as day that they have no right to the land and it is permissible to drive them out at will...."

Captain Harvey Brown made this sketch of Fort New Smyrna in 1839. The fort was located between the South Causeway Bridge and Andrews Street on South Riverside Drive.

Brown's sketch shows the eastern side of Fort Smyrna, facing the river. Six Doric columns of the Dunham mansion remained after the house was burned by Indians in 1835. The foundation of the mansion was recycled into Fort Smyrna.

The configuration of the stockade was similar to others of this war era: four log houses built in a hollow square. Two buildings were occupied by troops of the garrison, one by the officers, and the other served as a hospital and commissary.

During The War Between the States these ruins were again reused as a Confederate battery.

(Sketch courtesy of the Halifax Historical Society, Inc.)

Many forts were established throughout Florida during this period. One was begun in New Smyrna about 1836—abandoned and rebuilt several times. A post was maintained here in 1849, with "operations being wholly of a protective character." Fort New Smyrna was officially closed on November 10, 1853.

Illness was prevalent among the troops. New Smyrna statistics for Company B, Third Artillery note:

"Although the troops were well covered from the sun and rain they suffered greatly in the summer and fall months from intermittent fever. In 1840 the sick list comprised about two-thirds of the command, and the same season in 1841 *every* individual at the post was attacked sooner or later by the disease...."

Few escaped contracting malaria. "Officers as well as men...were the victims of the *malaria*...Assistant Surgeon Noyes, who left New Smyrna severely sick,

Fort Smyrna was located in the 400 block of South Riverside Drive near the South Causeway bridge.

died in St. Augustine shortly after his arrival July 26. Assistant Surgeon Weightman returned to St. Augustine completely broken down by *malaria* at New Smyrna, dropsy supervened, and he died October 30."

Retired surveyor and local historian Charles W. Bockelman pinpointed the site of Fort New Smyrna. Utilizing the 1884 field notes of surveyor Alfred Howard, he found the site described as an "old rebel battery."

Its location was 240 feet south of Lytle Avenue and 967 feet north of the Old Stone Wharf (in the Indian River North near Clinch Street and South Riverside Drive). For a comprehensive treatment of this era, the reader is referred to the posthumous publication of *Six Columns and Fort New Smyrna* by Charles W. Bockelman. The Halifax Historical Society, Inc. of Daytona Beach published this title under the editorship of Harold D. and Priscilla Cardwell, Sr.

THE DUNHAM MANSION GRACED OUR RIVERFRONT UNTIL 1835

Residents in the 400 block of South Riverside Drive may be surprised that their property was the site of Mary and Caroline Dunham's stately mansion with six pillars.

Caroline Dunham deeded Mary Dunham "100 acres of hammock or front land on the Hillsboro River on which last there is a large stone dwelling house" in April 1831.

This property was bounded by Canal Street on the north, Clinch Street on the south, east by the river, and west by Citron Avenue (west of the FEC Railway tracks).

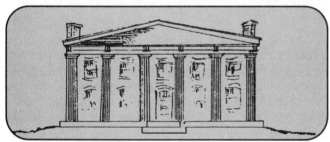

The Dunham mansion with Doric six columns stood in the 400 block of South Riverside Drive. Seminole Indians burned it on December 28, 1835. (Artist's sketch by Charles W. Bockelman)

The mansion and the rest of New Smyrna were burned by Indians on December 28, 1835. During the ensuing Second Seminole War (1835-42), its foundations and pillars were used for the US Army's Fort Smyrna from 1836-53.

Later, the ruins also served as a battery for Confederate troops who ambushed Union troops searching for blockade runners in 1862.

The Dunhams' sold this 100-acre parcel for $1,750 in January 1837 to two US Army paymasters, Colonel Christopher Andrews and Major John S. Lytle, who had discovered New Smyrna during the Second Seminole War. Even with the war in progress, Andrews and Lytle recognized a post-war real estate opportunity.

Jacob Motte, a US Army surgeon, kept a dairy from 1836-38, later entitled *Journey Into Wilderness*:

"In the midst of orange, lemon, fig, and other blossoming trees...there appeared the ruined columns, towering upwards, like gigantic sentries of the place, of Judge Dunham's once princely mansion; all that remained visible; the walls having been blown down as 'twas said by the explosion of a keg of powder, which unknown to the Indians who fired the building was concealed in the cellar....We pitched our tents amid the ruins...."

SEMINOLE INDIANS SET NEW SMYRNA ABLAZE

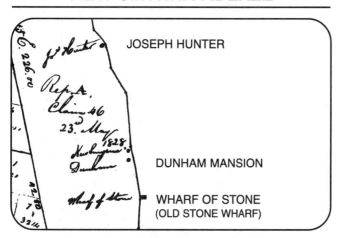

JOSEPH HUNTER

DUNHAM MANSION

WHARF OF STONE
(OLD STONE WHARF)

Three homesteads along the Indian River North are featured on this 1835 survey map. Joseph Hunter's was near the intersection of Faulkner Street and North Dixie Freeway.

John Sheldon managed the Cruger and Depeyster sugar mill. The Sheldons' house was on top of the coquina foundation in Old Fort Park. The Dunham mansion stood on South Riverside Drive between Andrews Street and Lytle Avenue.

Christmas Day 1835 brought disturbing news. Mrs. John D. Sheldon's maid had been to a party the night before at Joseph Hunter's sugar plantation about two miles north of the Sheldons' house.

The maid had seen nine Indians with painted faces. Painted faces meant trouble—war.

Only two months earlier, John and Jane Sheldon and her mother, Jane Murray, had moved to New Smyrna. He was placed in charge of the Cruger and Depeyster sugar mill facility. Now, fearing the worst, the Sheldons and the Hunters gathered a few belongings and crossed the river to Colonel Douglas Dummett's place on Mt. Pleasant (north of Marker 33 Condominium on South Indian River Road).

Their move was none too soon. At 1 a.m. on December 28, Judge Dunham's mansion was ablaze. A large group of Indians under Chief Philip, together with a small party of Uchees, and between 110 to 120 blacks (probably Indian slaves) were dancing around the fire.

When the mansion's roof collapsed, their yells were terrific. One account puts a keg of gunpowder in Dunham's cellar. Imagine the Indians' surprise when the gun powder exploded!

In the course of that day the Cruger and Depeyster dwelling house, outbuildings and the Sugar Mill were burned; negro slaves were captured and taken off. Three miles north, Joseph Hunter's cotton house was burnt and four or five negroes taken.

During their rampage, the Indians systematically destroyed New Smyrna. They set fire to nearly all of the buildings, Sugar Mill and neighboring plantations, and spared only the corn houses for their own use.

The refugees at Col. Dummett's watched New Smyrna's fiery skyline. Fearing the Indians would cross the river, they fled to Bulow plantation (Ormond Beach), where they waited for a military escort to St. Augustine.

This departure was also well timed; 11 Indians crossed the river about noon on December 28th. They laid waste to the plantation, then tried unsuccessfully to burn the house on Mt. Pleasant. All of Dummett's personal belongings were destroyed except two tables.

In addition, the Indians burnt the dwelling of Mr. Racliff, a little north of Col. Dummett's. Next they went to the newly completed lighthouse at the inlet. There they broke glass, destroyed the lantern, set fire to the lighthouse, and took the silver reflectors.

When Col. Dummett and his troops returned, they found the Indians had removed all the lead from the sugar boilers. No doubt, the salvaged lead would be used to mold bullets. Also, two kegs of rum were missing.

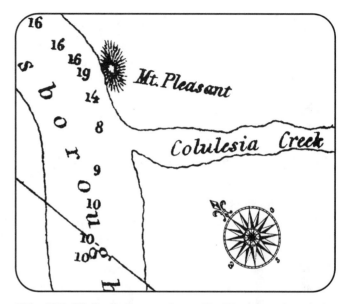

This 1851 US Coast Survey shows Mt. Pleasant, site of the Dummett homestead, two blocks south of Flagler Avenue. Indian shell mounds were prize real estate in Florida's pioneer days. If you built your house on top, you got better breezes with fewer mosquitoes and "no-seeums." You could also see who was coming to dinner. By 1900 these numerous mounds became ready sites for road bed material. All you needed was a wagon.

WHERE IS MASSACRE BLUFF?

Residents of Dune Circle, west of North Peninsula Avenue, will be surprised to learn their prominent elevation was once called "Massacre Bluff."

A French schooner wrecked half way between Cape Canaveral and New Smyrna in 1835. As shipwrecked sailors had done for centuries, eight to ten survivors began their long walk to the safety of St. Augustine.

Mosquito Inlet (renamed Ponce de Leon Inlet) barred their way. They searched for logs to make a raft.

Since the tide was on the ebb, they camped on a bluff. There they awaited morning and a more favorable tide to cross the inlet. Morning never came.

Their camp fire attracted Indians who crossed the river that night and massacred the entire party.

The tragic site was described in 1840 by a diarist who had been stationed at Fort New Smyrna at the beginning of the Second Seminole War:

"Our eyes were attracted by a little wooded bluff at our left, on the summit of which was a small paling, enclosing graves, as we were told, of some murdered seamen who had been found there and buried by our troops."

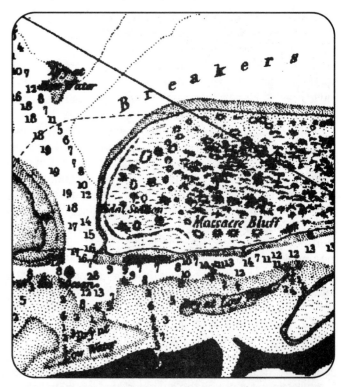

1851 US Coast Survey, Mosquito Inlet, Sketch F No. 3 shows the inlet channel and the south (New Smyrna) peninsula.

Definitely used as a Sugar Mill in the 1830's, was this elegant structure actually built during an earlier period? As some claim, was it really an ancient Spanish mission "recycled" into a sugar mill?
From Adolph Wittemann's *Florida*, 1885

1894 engraving from
the *New York Herald*

DID CHRISTOPHER COLUMBUS BUILD THE SUGAR MILL?

Northern newspapers have always had a flair for the fantastic when relating events in the South. The above engraving comes from the Sunday, March 4, 1894, issue of the *New York Herald*. The accompanying headline is worthy of those weekly tabloids displayed at any supermarket check-out line:

MAY BE AMERICA'S OLDEST BUILDING
Picturesque Ruins of a Venerable
and Mysterious Structure
in South Florida.
WAS IT ERECTED BY COLUMBUS?

The article quotes former New Smyrna Mayor Rev. J.A. Ball concerning the evident religious nature of the architecture. He surmised this coquina structure was a mission built during Christopher Columbus' extended second expedition in 1493.

Perhaps the popular World's Columbian Exposition in Chicago during 1893 set the stage for this historical fantasy. It did not go unchallenged.

Florida historian George Fairbanks responded with "a conclusive refutation" almost immediately. Positively, the ruin was a sugar mill from the nineteenth century.

Likewise, renown author and historian Woodbury Lowery dismissed this junk history: "The article chiefly consists of purely gratuitous assumptions concerning questions which have never even been in dispute."

Although the Columbus chapel connection may have disappeared thereafter, the Spanish Mission/Sugar Mill controversy did not.

In May 1893, New York stock broker Washington E. Connor purchased a 10-acre site including the Spanish Mission/Sugar Mill from Isadora Matthews for $400.

In 1914, Connor gave the picturesque ruins as a birthday present to his second wife and new bride, Jeanette Thurber Connor.

Mrs. Connor became an authority on Florida's early Spanish history, and with John B. Stetson, Jr., founded the Florida Historical Society. She made extensive studies and translations from over 100,000 photostatted pages from the Archive of the Indies at Seville, Spain. Her works include a definitive biography of Pedro Menendez de Aviles and two volumes of a proposed 10-volume set of *Colonial Records of Florida*, to cover the Spanish occupation from 1570 to 1700.

Sugar Mill south arches about 1920

Mrs. Connor's research indicated three missions built of coquina were constructed south of St. Augustine by Franciscan monks and Indians. They were located along the coast, nine leagues from each other. The missions were named St. Josef, Tissimi and Atocuimi.

Atocuimi was the mission at New Smyrna.

These missions, she claimed, were founded to serve the Jororo Indians (pronounced Ho-ro-ro) and were first mentioned in Spanish documents in 1690. In addition to ministering to the Jororos' spiritual needs, the Franciscans taught the Indians construction techniques and how to clear and cultivate the land.

In 1693 the Franciscans appealed to the King of Spain for funds. In 1696, they received 200 large hoes, six large saws and six small ones, 50 machetes, four large augers, four medium sized and four gimlets. Three missions south of St. Augustine were apparently built with these tools. Eight monks supervised construction.

Dedicated as San Joseph de Jororo, the mission was constructed about 1696, according to Mrs. Connor. The Jororo Indians and their missions were burned in 1706 during the second invasion of Florida by Governor James Moore of South Carolina, who was aided by Creek Indians. An epidemic in 1727 decimated the surviving Jororos.

THREE BRONZE CANDLESTICKS FOUND AT SUGAR MILL IN 1881

The Sugar Mill ruins are located on a 77-acre tract Captain Emanuel J. Matthews' received from the US Government in 1878.

Matthews was clearing an area near the foundations for a patch of turnips. There he unearthed a number of metal objects in 1881. The remains of three bronze candlesticks—such as those used in Roman Catholic services—were uncovered. This suggested a more ancient history for the site known to have been used for a sugar mill in the early 1830's and burned by the Indians in 1835.

During his 1925 journey to Spain, John Y. Detwiler searched cathedrals for replicas of the New Smyrna candlesticks. He carried an enlargement of the accompanying photograph. No replicas were found.

The main difference was in the square base of the candlestick. Those Detwiler viewed in Spain were triangular, emblematic of the Holy Trinity.

"The parts of three Bronze Candlesticks, found in the Old Mission near New Smyrna, have been proved to be of Moorish origin, having square bases, emblematic of the materialist elements of earth, air, fire and water—words which would indicate an antiquity even greater than the discovery of America, or the conquest of Moorish possessions by Spain....in repairing the cathedral in Seville shortly after the Moorish conquest, every effort was made to eradicate the materialistic emblems embodied in the square, typifying earth, air, fire, water. In the case of the candlesticks it was only necessary to loosen the rod, remove the base, supply it with another of triangular form, and the work was done.

"Is not the conclusion evident that at that early day the candlesticks captured in the Moorish mosques had not yet come under the censure of the ecclesiastical authorities?" Detwiler hypothesized.

Other authorities claimed the candlesticks were of American Colonial origin. The candlesticks were donated to the Florida Historical Society. In a 1908 "Catalog of Collections" they are listed as "Fragments of bronze candlesticks found at ruins of old Spanish mission near New Smyrna."

DEBUNKING THE SO-CALLED SPANISH MISSION RUINS

One story often leads to another. Charles H. Coe founded the *Florida Star,* the first newspaper south of St. Augustine, in 1877. The 21-year-old journeyman printer produced the 16-page monthly journal four miles west of New Smyrna. Once the location of a small community, Glencoe Road still bears part of Coe's family name.

Debunking the So-Called Spanish Mission Near New Smyrna was a 32-page booklet Coe published in 1941.

"This fanciful idea was first advanced by Washington E. Connor. The reason for his belief was centered in the arches used in the walls in place of regular doors and windows. He thought that such masonry was too elaborate for a sugar-mill," Coe launched into his debunking treatise.

Coquina was used because it was the best and cheapest material at hand. The Sugar Mill engine room was of "identical

Could this live oak growing through the drying room floor date these ruins?

character and material in general as the other construction. Perhaps it is a little more finished, as this building, with its costly machinery, was the most valuable part of the Sugar-Mill, and probably was the first to be built....Its measurements, too, indicate an English origin."

Coe first saw the ruins in 1874: "The coquina of which the ruins were built was quite fresh and clean. Moss or other accumulations due to the passage of time were scarcely visible. It did not require an expert builder or stonemason to realize that the entire building was of comparatively recent construction....Compared to the ancient and weather worn fort at St. Augustine, this masonry was of yesterday."

If Indians had inhabited and helped contruct the site, artifacts would have been uncovered. None have been found.

However, the most obvious testimony remains unheard, its evidence unexplored: "A large growing live oak tree, 11 feet in circumference [in 1941], is in the Sugar-Drying Room. This silent but significant witness undoubtedly approximates the true age of the ruins."

Coe spent three years researching several hundred books, documents and almost 100 early Florida maps to reach his conclusions.

However, archaeology had yet to enter into the investigation. It wasn't until 1950 when archaeologist John W. Griffin surveyed the site for the Florida Board of Parks and Historical Memorials.

"We found no aboriginal remains and no Spanish artifacts. The 'chapel' exactly matched the machinery house at the nearby Bulow plantation [in Flagler County]," Griffin reported.

Furthermore, all the measurements of the New Smyrna mill were English Standard, and the mill was not built on Spanish foundations. The ruins dated to the early 1800's and belonged to sugar plantations of the Second Spanish and Territorial periods.

Construction of the Sugar Mill was begun in 1830 by William Kemble who was contracted by William Depeyster and Eliza and Henry N. Cruger of New York.

The land was purchased from the estate of Ambrose Hull in two parcels: 500 acres of hammock land surrounding the Sugar Mill and 100 acres on the riverfront, surrounding the Old Fort Park site. The deal included "the steam engines, machinery, utensils and implements, wagons, carts and carriages, horses, mules, also the negro slaves and cattle."

Henry Cruger was empowered to manage, lease, mortgage, sell or otherwise dispose the plantation. It was operated by Thomas Stamps, a South Carolina sugar planter. Shortly after its completion, the seven-year Seminole War began. The Sugar Mill was burned along with the rest of New Smyrna on December 28, 1835.

The Connors conveyed the site to the Florida State Park Service in 1928. Today the park is managed by Volusia County and is open daily for visitors. This hideaway park is a must-see site. Bring your camera.

If you blink, you might miss it. This is the unassuming entrance to the Sugar Mill at 600 Old Mission Road. It is 3/10 mile south from the intersection of Mission Drive and SR 44 at K-Mart.

ANCIENT SPANISH MISSI
NEW SMY

1890

1910

1900

1920

North pier

The Old Stone Wharf was the center of town in the 1770's. One of Turnbull's first public works in New Smyrna, this coquina wharf is best seen at low tide west of Marker 42. Bottles, ballast stones, bronze ship nails, bullets, and a cannonball from the 1863 Union bombardment of New Smyrna have been found at this historic location.

Two piers, made of blocks averaging 20" x 30" x 8", are 45' apart and extend into the river over 80'. The blocks are set into the shell bank along South Riverside Drive, immediately north of Clinch Street. A coquina monument and plaque erected by the Daughters of the American Revolution marks the site.

REBELS WIN 1862 SKIRMISH AT THE OLD STONE WHARF

A skirmish occurred near the Old Stone Wharf between the 3rd Florida Regiment and sailors from the Union steamers on March 22, 1862. Based on the concentration of bullets and buttons discovered by Ray Goodrich, the actual battle may have occurred 100 yards north of the Old Stone Wharf.

The stage for inevitable conflict had been set. The Union fleet was already patrolling the Florida coast, looking for blockade runners headed to Nassau or Cuba. In addition, two Union steamers, the *Henry Andrews* and the *Penguin* had been sent to protect 2,000 feet of red cedar and 40,000 feet of live oak timber stored on the north peninsula along the Halifax River.

New Smyrna was well located to become one of the busiest blockade running ports in the South. Goods were brought from Europe to Nassau, landed at New Smyrna and transported by wagon to the St. Johns River.

Even small boats carrying one bale of cotton met larger ships, contributing to the blockade running effort. Cotton was exchanged for quinine, needles, coffee, piece-cloth, medicine, and other essential supplies.

Meanwhile, two companies of the 3rd Florida Regiment under command of Captain Daniel Bird, Company E and Captain Matthew Strain of Company H were in New Smyrna to take charge of an expected shipment of arms and supplies brought from the Bahamas. They also guarded stores of cotton, hidden in sheds west of the wharf, awaiting export. This is how Cottonshed Avenue (today Inwood Avenue) got its name.

Early on Saturday morning, March 22, 1862, nine small boats with approximately 43 Union troops and a four-pound howitzer headed south along the Indian River North toward Mosquito Lagoon. They had information that the *Kate*, a small sailing craft, was attempting to evade the blockade.

The *Kate* was found abandoned. They left 12 men aboard. Returning late that afternoon, the sailors relaxed their vigilance; they were within sight of *Henry Andrew*.

However, their passage had not gone unnoticed by the Confederate forces hidden along the banks near the Old Stone Wharf. Two of the boats drew nearer to examine the apparently deserted earthwork.

This "earthwork," located in the 400 block of South Riverside Drive, was the foundation of Dunham's mansion used as Fort Smyrna during the Second Seminole War (see pages 53-56).

The south pier of the Old Stone Wharf is north of Clinch Street.

The Third Florida Regiment's 1862 skirmish with Union sailors was first reenacted in 1983.

OUR FIRST TRAGEDY OF WAR BEGINS AT THE OLD STONE WHARF

***New Smyrna The Beautiful*, published in 1904 by A.E. Dumble, provides this account of the skirmish:**

On they came, unsuspicious of danger, and as the two launches with the two officers touched the shore, Captain Strain fired, killing Lt. Budd instantly. We then opened fire upon the astonished enemy and at the first fire all the occupants of the two first launches were killed, except two wounded and one Negro pilot, who temporarily escaped unhurt.

The remaining launches pulled for the opposite shore under a hot fire from our men, and several were killed and wounded before they reached the mangrove swamp on the opposite side of the river. The boats were brought in next morning, and all were partly filled with blood, showing that great damage had been done. One of the launches had a four-pound howitzer on board, but its fire was ineffectual.

The two launches in which all were killed or wounded, drifted some distance from the shore, and Tom O'Neil, a good-natured Irishman, asked leave to swim out and bring them in. This was granted, and O'Neil did so.

Reenactment Union troops land at the Old Stone Wharf.

On reaching the boat on which were Captain Mather and his crew, he made it fast to the other launch and then got aboard.

He found a five-gallon keg of whiskey in one of the boats and, being like most Irishmen, fond of a drop of the crayther, turned it up and took a long, strong pull at the keg, and could not be prevailed upon to come ashore until he had repeated the performance several times. So when he drifted away, he was happy as could be. The Negro pilot had also drifted away. He lay down and tried to work the oar with one foot.

One of our men asked permission to fire, and shot through the Negro's ankle. He was brought in, suffering greatly, and was guarded until next morning, when he was taken to Glencoe and hung. The two wounded men were made as comfortable as circumstances would allow. One of them, a stalwart sailor, was shot through the calf of the leg. He suffered greatly and died in a short time. He had no nerve. The other, a small Swede, was shot from his shoulder to his knee with 12 to 15 Enfield bullets. He never groaned. Although unable to move, he bore his suffering without a word, and strange to say, recovered.

The gold watches of the officers were, with letters from their wives, etc., returned under a flag of truce. The dead were taken to the edge of the hammock and placed in one grave, officers on the bottom and the men above, eight in all.

Seven were wounded and taken prisoners. The bodies of the officers were delivered under a flag of truce the next morning to a party from the gunboats.

Thus was enacted the first tragedy of the great war on the shores of New Smyrna.

Reenactment troops gather under the Cannonball Oak in Old Fort Park (2001). A Union shell fired in 1863 lodged in this live oak. Rest assured, schoolboys recovered it shortly thereafter.

Detail of stamp

Philatelists will recognize this rare New Smyrna overprint, currently worth over $45,000. A five-cent Confederate stamp was to be overprinted with "10" to double its value. The typesetter mistakenly set his numerals left to right, instead of right to left, which printed as "01."

A black border on this patriotic cover addressed to "Miss Jenny Johnston" meant news of a death.

ARE CONFEDERATE RIFLES BURIED DOWNTOWN?

Are Confederate rifles buried near downtown New Smyrna Beach? Here's a letter sent to the Chamber of Commerce, then at 305 Canal Street. Secretary William Behne received this letter in September 1924 from Mrs. Eva Scott of Quitman, Georgia.

"My father was a Confederate soldier, one of the first to volunteer in the First Florida Regiment at Monticello. They were sent to south Florida to guard the coast and were stationed at New Smyrna.

"As long as he lived, he never tired of telling what a time they had there. He said at the time—in 1861—the woods were full of all kinds of game, as well as a natural growth of butter and lima beans and also what they called 'bird's-eye pepper.'

"They could get fish, too, and lived well while there. They found sweet potatoes that had not been killed by the frosts in years. He would have been a great booster for your back-country.

"He's been dead four years [1920], but while living was forever wanting to go back to New Smyrna. One thing he said he wanted to go for was to dig for his old war gun.

"The way he told about it was this: the Yankees came in on them unawares and before they would let them get their arms, they stacked them and buried them in one deep hole which they had dug right on a blackjack ridge in sight of New Smyrna. He said he could find the spot if he went there.

"His regiment was ordered to Mississippi and he never knew whether the guns were ever found. He believed until he died that they were still there, and they may be, but believe me they would be right in town now. But wouldn't I appreciate his gun, if it could be found! Possibly it bears his name: James E. Scott.

"I love Florida; I was born there and hope some day to go back. Look for Daddy's gun for me."

> The War Between the States may have ended at Appomattox in 1865, but it was not forgotten. Victoria Sheldon met a Yankee veteran at a dance in New Smyrna. He had lost one hand in battle. After their introduction she remarked, "It's certainly a pleasure to meet a Yankee who has been trimmed to my satisfaction."

PAY BACK: NEW SMYRNA BOMBED AND BURNED BY UNION TROOPS

The loss of seven Union sailors at the Old Stone Wharf was humiliating enough. A month later, on April 27, 1862, the crew of the *Henry Andrew* watched live oak timber and 2,000 feet of cedar burn brightly just north of the lighthouse. This was the same timber they had been instructed to guard. Although Yankee retribution was over 16 months in coming, it arrived with full force and fury one Sunday morning.

Two ships came up the river on July 26, 1863, toward the Sheldon hotel atop Old Fort Park mound. Noon day meal preparations continued. It was probably just Yankees searching for small ships loading cotton, waiting to slip through their naval blockade.

"Assurance had been given civilians that their homes would not be invaded," was the official decree, although a patrolling vessel had lobbed three shots across the peninsula from the ocean on July 9 and 11. Today, July 26, the steamer US *Oleander* with the schooner *Beauregard* in tow came closer and swung broadside.

"Before coming to anchor, and strangely enough, without the notice prescribed in the 'Regulations,' fire was opened upon Shell Hill. The puff of white smoke and the shell whistling above the house was the first intimation its inmates had of danger. It was noon, and dinner was being prepared, but now all fled to the hammock, going in a northerly direction to evade the line of fire. The family consisted of Mrs. Sheldon and six children, one of whom, Victoria, was married and had with her two children, one a baby in arms—eighteen all told, not counting numerous servants," A.E. Dumble recounts in *New Smyrna The Beautiful,* published in 1904.

"As a point of safety, they made a camp in the dense forest and built a fire. This was in the hottest season of the year, and the jungle was alive with mosquitoes and sandflies. Their situation was indeed most pitiable. They could hear the bursting shells, many of which searched the woods near them, the smoke from their fire having been discovered. There was nothing to be done.

"Too weary to go further, their only hope was to remain hidden. Fortunately, a rain having set in, the firing ceased for a time, and the married daughter, Victoria, and R.S. Sheldon, then a lad of 17, stole back to the house. They found the dinner on the stove and the silver on the table, but the house itself was riddled by shot and shell. The prepared food, the silverware, or as much of it as could be caught up, together with a few trifles, were packed up and carried into the forest.

"Many of the shells and shot had gone completely through the house; some of the shells had burst in and over it. Everywhere was ruin. Tables, chairs, pictures, many old family heirlooms, precious beyond price, lay shattered and in chaotic confusion. The great oak west of the house and one hundred and fifty feet away, had been struck in the upper massive trunk, leaving a great wound plainly visible at this day. The fugitives hurried out of the west doorway, keeping the doomed buildings between them and the boats.

"Firing was kept up every half-hour during the night. At ten the next morning crews landed from the vessels and completed their mission by setting fire to the house. And now Mrs. Sheldon, who had in years gone by watched the savages burn her house and destroy all she possessed, once more saw the black smoke of destruction rising from her home.

"In the cellar of the house a quantity of gunpowder had been buried. This finally exploded, throwing down the large stone chimney and scattering debris for long distances. The runaways heard the ominous roar that told them all was done. The second and last tragedy of the great war had been enacted on Shell Hill."

Part of the "Old Fort" foundation was visible when John D. Sheldon built his 50-room hotel in 1859. He used this as a cellar for his hotel.

Viewing the foundation in Old Fort Park today, you can see the northeast corner wall of his "cellar" has been extensively rebuilt, using smaller pieces of unshaped coquina. Possibly this was the wall damaged by the gunpowder explosion during the 1863 bombardment.

From the Union flagship *Wabash* of the South Atlantic Blockading Squadron, Flag Officer S. DuPont commanding, directed the bombardment and burning of New Smyrna.

"HOUSE ON THE HILL" WAS BUILT ON "OLD FORT" FOUNDATIONS

An Indian shell mound was a prize piece of real estate in early Florida. Your house had better drainage, less chance of flooding, great view, and access to more breezes to help the mosquitoes on their way.

John D. Sheldon bought 25 acres (bounded by Canal and Washington streets) from Thomas Stamps on June 23, 1854 for $750. Completed in 1859, the Sheldons' 50-room hotel was built with dressed lumber brought from the North. It was the largest hotel south of St. Augustine.

John D. Sheldon died in August 1862 of yellow fever. Less than a year later the hotel was leveled in a Union bombardment (see page 72). His widow Jane and the children built another hotel. Years later she described The War Between the States as bringing her "the sorest trials and greatest sorrows of my life."

Son R.S. Sheldon recalled, "In the fall of 1865, we came back and built a smaller house on the same site. It was made largely of wreck timber picked up on the beach; the floor was of puncheon, hewn plank split from logs; the shingles were split out and shaved with a

John D. Sheldon
1807-1862

Jane Murray Sheldon
1813-1903

Welcome to the Sheldons' homestead/hotel 1898

A lone chimney stands sentinel in the Sheldon house after its demolition in 1903. Note the "Old Fort" foundations exposed.

drawing knife on a draw horse. For some years it was the only house on the present site of New Smyrna."

Although it was neither as large nor as elaborate as the pre-war hotel, it became a pioneer "shopping center." Besides boarding rooms, it housed Sheldon and Childs' general store, post office, port collector's office, shoe shop, and a print shop where Charles William Coe published this area's first newspaper, *The Florida Star*, in 1877. The "Lean Too" (at the right) served as the dining room. This hotel was torn down about 1903.

After the death of Jane Sheldon on June 7, 1903, the property was sold to John T. Hammond, a local banker and investor. Hammond was the first to begin extensive excavations on this curious landmark, which revealed the foundations of three western rooms and four corner buttresses. He also built the coquina retaining wall and steps around the foundation on Julia Street and North Riverside Drive.

These excavations unearthed many Indian relics, almost all from the St. Johns Period (500 A.D.). Hammond sold the property to Captain F.W. Sams, which then passed to daughter Anne Sams Bouchelle. Later, the property was cleared, with excavation help from A.S. Robinson who uncovered "the entire plan of the fort—showing steps, two rooms and so on—the existence of which has hitherto been only a surmise."

"New Smyrna. This small settlement of half a dozen houses...is reached by a rather rough-traveling weekly stage from Enterprise, for the immoderate sum of $8.00 a head. Board can be obtained of Mrs. Sheldon."

A Guide-Book of Florida and the South for Tourists, Invalids and Emigrants
by Daniel G. Brinton, M.D. 1869.

Under an $17,400 Work Projects Administration (WPA) grant in 1937, 21 workers excavated the ruins, squared up the coquina blocks and rebuilt the northeast wall. Some WPA workmen saw the "likeness" of the date 1529 on one of the newly exposed corners, according to the March 6, 1936, issue of the *New Smyrna Times.*

The next day the *Daytona Beach Observer* reported: "A date of 1519 believed to have been chiseled into the north side of the outside foundation of the old fort at New Smyrna may affect the history of the United States.

"City prisoners, who for several months have been clearing ground on the old fort hill and gradually unearthing the old fort, uncovered the rock on which the old date is inscribed.

"According to history, the old fort, uncovered for the first time several years ago, is presumed to be the fort mentioned in the diary of Mendoza, a Spanish priest, who made a voyage to Florida with Menedez, and is believed to have been built by Menendez in 1565.

"The new date, however, indicates the fort might have been built by Portuguese who roamed the country before either Menendez or Ponce de Leon. Although de Leon came to Florida for the first time in 1513, according to history, and again in 1539, it is not believed he started the building of any forts in Florida," the *Observer* said.

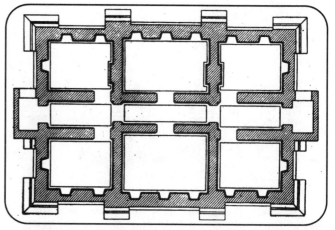

The massive "Old Fort" has baffled investigators for over a century. Although the Sheldons knew their house was built on this curious foundation, the opportunity for excavation occurred after 1903 when their house/hotel was torn down.

A.S. Robinson's scale drawing (above) of the 55 x 86' structure includes a series of imagined doorways connecting the nine "cellar" compartments.

During the Old Fort's WPA reconstruction, New Smyrna City Engineer Harry Bonnet calculated 400 cubic yards of masonry in the foundation. Given 50 men for 12-16 hours per day, it would take two-and-a-half months to duplicate this structure.

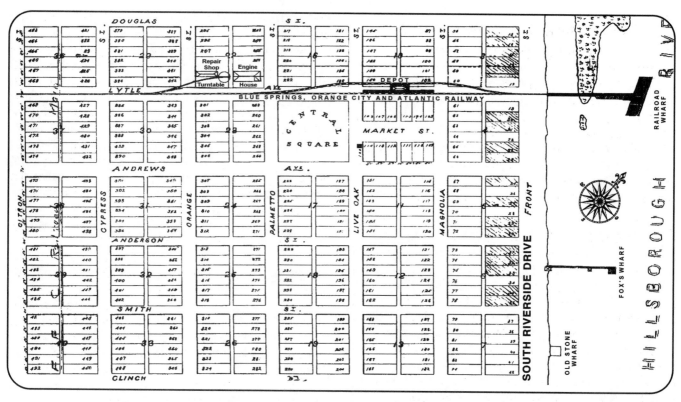

1888 SURVEY — SOUTHERN PORTION OF THE 100-ACRE R.S. ANDREWS SUBDIVISION

WELCOME TO DOWNTOWN NEW SMYRNA 1888

New Smyrna's original "downtown" was not Canal Street. Activity was centered around the Blue Spring, Orange City and Atlantic Railway (BSOCA) which ran down Lytle Avenue to a steamboat wharf north of Riverside Apartments, 408 South Riverside Drive.

This first business district was situated along Riverside Drive (then called Front Street). It prospered briefly until Henry Flagler's Florida East Coast Railway (FEC) arrived in New Smyrna in 1892. The FEC was deeded the BSOCA Railway in 1896.

As shown in the accompanying 1888 survey, the entire city block bounded by Lytle Avenue and Live Oak, Andrews and Palmetto streets was reserved as a "Central Square" for municipal buildings. Until the late 1930's New Smyrna's City Hall, Police Department, Fire Department, jail, and a zoo were in the Central Square.

Today Bert Fish Medical Center occupies this site and two more city blocks to the south. The current hospital parking lot bounded by Live Oak and Magnolia streets was originally divided by a 100-foot wide "Market Street" faced with twelve 50 x 100' storefronts. However, with the demise of the BSOCA Railway, this business district never happened.

By 1900 commercial properties on Canal Street were being developed and was destined to become our main business district.

This 100-acre parcel known as the R. Snowden Andrews Subdivision represents New Smyrna's first taste of city planning. Its "urban" plan encompassed everything east of the FEC railroad tracks from Canal Street to Clinch Street. One of its more practical features is a series of alleyways, which keep parking, deliveries and garbage pickup off the main streets.

RIVERSIDE DRIVE HAS SEVERAL ALIASES

It was Front Street in 1879, then Hillsborough or Hillsboro Street by 1895—folks here were flexible spellers who believed in elegant variation. It became North and South Riverside Drive after World War II.

South of Clinch Street (1916) was originally called "Palm Avenue" because the Rio Vista Hotel (today the Indian River Lodge & Conference Center, 1210 South Riverside Drive) was on the outskirts of town. The hotel built its own access road, which was later deeded to the city and became South Riverside Drive.

FIRST TRAIN ARRIVES IN 1887

Contrary to what you might expect, New Smyrna's first railway connection did not come from the north, but from the west. Begun in 1881 by Orange City merchant W.W. West, this first train in Volusia County carried oranges and an occasional passenger. Originally, it ran from Orange City to Blue Spring Landing.

The remaining 28.4-mile line reached New Smyrna in 1887 and the Blue Spring, Orange City and Atlantic Railway (BSOCA) was born. Facetiously called "Built Strictly On Credit and Air," its standard-gauge tracks ran down the north side of Lytle Avenue. The depot was between Live Oak and Magnolia streets. A railroad wharf allowed shipment of oranges by boat (see page 78).

A railroad line coming into any town meant prosperity. Helen DeLand, for whom the town of Lake Helen was named, recalled the event in West Volusia:

"When the train pulled in—such hustling! All scurried aboard the flat cars on which were planks or boards supported by wooden blocks for seats, then toward New Smyrna. Streams of smoke and sparks settled on 'we uns' and kept us busy putting out the fires that started on our clothes. Cattle and hogs disputed the right of way and the engine kept tooting to frighten them off. One long-horn refused to leave the track and at last the train slowed to a snail's pace and at that pushed the critter off into the ditch, heels up....At New Smyrna there was a grand feast and orations."

Meanwhile, New Smyrna's Mrs. R.S. Sheldon described the arrival of the first train: "The countryside was covered with people who had walked, ridden horseback, in carts, buggies and wagons for miles and miles to see that first train. Bands were playing and people were shouting as the train came in, pulling a string of cars behind it. People shouted in joy."

Our first railroad connection came from the west. Its wharf would be in the shadow of the South Causeway bridge today.

Flagler's East Coast Railway arrived in 1892. Originally, the passenger station was on the east side of the racks. After 1906 the station was moved to the west side (note the location of the water tower in the distance).

In 1925 a nearly $2 million repair facility was opened here with nine pits, turntable and roundhouse. About 250 workers were employed. They handled five engines per month for complete repairs and up to 75 engines per day for running repairs. At its peak, there was a train through New Smyrna every hour, day or night.

Indeed, New Smyrna was a railroad town. Every family had someone (or everyone) working for the FEC Railway. The economic impact of a railroad strike could easily be predicted.

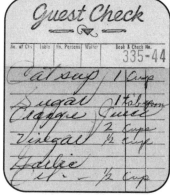

The FEC administrative offices were upstairs (top left); the ever-popular East Coast Restaurant was on the first floor. There were no menus; a chalkboard told it all. This recipe for the house salad dressing (using the secret ingredient orange juice) was passed along by a helpful waitress to Evelyn Beckham.

The 148 was the FEC's last steam locomotive commissioned.

Are we on time? Engineer Frank Bell Olcott checks his watch.

NOTICE TO THE PUBLIC

FLORIDA EAST COAST RAILWAY COMPANY
IS OPERATED UNDER STRIKE CONDITIONS

Use Premises and Ride Trains at Own Risk

Picket lines formed and the longest unresolved labor dispute in US history began on January 23, 1963.

After the strike began, FEC trains didn't move for ten days. On the eleventh day supervisory personnel ran a train from Jacksonville to Miami and back, defying the union. Negotiations, legal and political maneuvers continued while over 200 crimes against FEC property were committed. There were several wrecks in 1963; however, the 1964 bombing of two trains brought the wrath of President Lyndon Johnson who was within 15 miles of one of the explosions. Within three weeks, the FBI arrested four former FEC employees.

Subdued violence continued. When the Federal Government intervention showed strikers that violence would not be tolerated, 700 employees were back at work by late 1964. Others, still unreconciled, are on strike to this day.

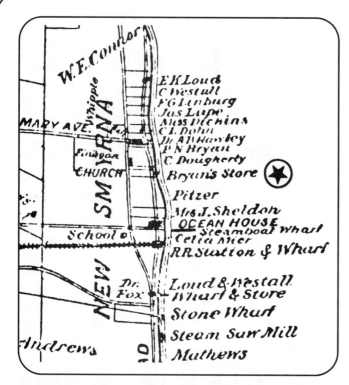

Here is the riverfront portion of New Smyrna's 1886 town survey by Alfred Howard prior to its incorporation on June 6, 1887.

1893-1903 CITY COUNCIL: THE UNCENSORED MINUTES

It was a long first day when New Smyrna incorporated on June 6, 1887. The meeting began at 10:00 a.m. and didn't adjourn until 7:30 p.m. Twenty-seven registered voters met at Bryan's Hall above Bryan's Store, located at Washington Street and North Riverside Drive (shown by the star on the 1886 survey).

Philemon N. Bryan was the unanimous choice for New Smyrna's first mayor. A.B. Hawley was elected President of the Council; other members included Christopher Westall, Frank W. Sams, John A. Ball, and George R. Pitzer. C.L. Dohn became Town Clerk; Milton Bryan, Town Treasurer; C.R. Dilzer, Town Collector; and J.R. Finegan, Town Assessor.

Any record of the first six years of council minutes is missing. Perhaps lost—or more likely, never officially recorded—the first minutes of New Smyrna City Council meetings begin in October 17, 1893. Curiously, at this meeting Councilman J.L. Rush motioned "to procure a minute or record book." The original police docket, however, begins four years earlier. After all, every town has to get its priorities in order.

TOWN MARSHAL GETS BUSTED

It's enough to make any lawman blush. At the first recorded New Smyrna City Council meeting, the Town Marshal was charged with:

(1) Malconduct and mal-administration;
(2) Intoxication while on duty, one or more instances;
(3) Allowing arrested persons to escape;
(4) Arresting, imprisoning and releasing persons without reporting to the Mayor;
(5) Unlawful seizure and retaining prisoners' effects.

Marshal Root acknowledged "having been remiss in the performances of his duties." The five charges were "in the main true" and he asked the Council for leniency. He promised he "would endeavor in the future to comply with his lawful duties."

Root was reinstated by unanimous vote.

However, old habits must have been hard to shake and shadowed Root. A second complaint surfaced a year later. During the December 1894 meeting it was revealed the Town Marshal "had been in the habit of using intoxicating liquors to excess while on duty."

Investigations (lengthy, one would surmise) followed and Root was discharged on December 28, 1895. Lewis Pallicer was elected as new Town Marshal and Collector.

City Council's first recorded meetings in 1893 were held at Dohn's Hall above Dohn's Livery. The livery stood on the west corner of Canal and Faulkner streets (201 Canal Street). Rent was $3.00 per month. In 1895 meetings moved to the Smith Building, now the BellSouth facility, 100 Canal Street.

Dohn's Hall was also home for Masonic Lodge 149 from its formation in 1896 until the livery building burned in 1905.

URGENT NEED IN 1894: LET'S BUILD A JAIL

First, you incorporate the town. Next thing you know, you need a jail. Mayor J.A. Ball stressed the "urgent need" for such a facility.

A motion passed to "secure plans and specifications for the proposed jail." Then reality arrived: large or small, all public works require money.

Councilman J.L. Rush reported the awful truth at the January 23, 1894 meeting: "The Money on hand is entirely too little to justify the town to build" a jail.

According to Volusia County Sheriff's Office Russ Galbreath, the first jail had a waterfront view. It was a converted shed on the Blue Spring, Orange City and Atlantic Railway wharf at the foot of Lytle Avenue (see pages 78 and 80).

The "urgent need" was postponed for seven years until January 18, 1901, when the city accepted the $141 low bid of C.H. Clark to build a 20 x 24-foot jail.

The specifications called for the "walls of building to be 12 feet high with four openings, three windows and one door in which grates are to be placed. Council to furnish grates and door."

Usually, more people are the cause of more crime. However, New Smyrna's population dropped from 600 in 1895 to 550 in 1901.

THEY WERE WILD IN THE STREETS

It seems like something out of the Wild West, but it must've been a problem here. Councilmen approved an ordinance making it unlawful "unless legally authorized to discharge by shooting any firearms within, into or across any street within the city limits of the town."

The fine was "not less than two dollars nor more than $10, or not less than one day nor more than five days imprisonment for each offense, at the discretion of the Mayor."

PAY-AS-YOU-GO POLICE AND PRINTING

It was a novel concept. Special policemen appointed at the April 3, 1894 session were expected to "serve without pay except for actual service rendered."

At this same cost-cutting meeting, Councilman R.S. Sheldon was instructed to "confer with the printer and secure, if possible, a reduction in rates for the town's printing for the ensuing year."

THE 1894 TAX MAN COMETH

Councilman J.L. Rush visited the County Assessor to get New Smyrna property valuations. On October 4, 1894, "10 mills upon the dollar of valuation was adopted as the amount of tax to be levied upon taxable property within the corporate limits for the year A.D. 1894."

Indian shell mounds were handy sources for roadbed fill.

WHERE DID ALL THE SHELL MOUNDS GO?

A recurrent entry in old council minutes concerns road repair. Such maintenance required vast quantities of shell, and what easier source than the 22 Indian shell mounds throughout our area.

It was hard labor; New Smyrna usually put its prison population to work. When there were no prisoners, the city paid—but not much. In 1893 two men for two weeks were authorized to "clear up the streets at a cost not exceeding $1.25 for each man employed."

A subscription list of black residents offered six days labor for the purpose of cleaning and grubbing Dora Avenue from Washington Avenue to Mary Avenue. Council approved $16 payment. Opening Ball Street cost $19.30; cleaning and ditching Mary Avenue to the corporate line was estimated at $136.50 in 1897.

S.H. Raulerson furnished and spread 900 cubic yards of shell on New Smyrna's streets for 60 cents per cubic yard in 1897. By 1901 the city's appetite for shell was up to 2,000 cubic yards at the inflated price of 70 cents per cubic yard.

Despite all this expensive shelling, the city obviously missed one hole. F.P. Zig found it and sought "damages sustained from driving into a hole in the street" on December 3, 1901.

Indian shell mounds that stood centuries before Christopher Columbus sailed were disappearing quickly. By 1903 the high price of shell was on everyone's mind.

The Street Committee's C. Murray reported he was "unable to secure shell for 60 cents per cubic yard as in the past, as the price at the mound was not 35 cents per cubic yard." The city wound up paying 75 cents per cubic yard of shell spread that year.

SPANISH AMERICA WAR SCARE

City council held a special session with Colonel Praskey to procure arms and ammunition from the Governor of the State of Florida.

The weapons were to be used in the protection of New Smyrna and vicinity in the event of invasion by the Spaniards.

The city was required to post a $2,000 bond for the safe return of 100 weapons.

IT'S A DIRTY JOB, BUT SOMEONE, ETC.

Did the Town Marshal wear too many hats? He was responsible for collecting license fees, dog collar badge fees, and was frequently told to have selected potholes in the street fixed.

As a bonus, he was also expected "to make the usual house-to-house sanitary inspection during the months of July, August and September."

For a job that paid $25 per month, his job description kept getting longer and more miscellaneous. The last straw came on May 12, 1898: "The Town Marshal was instructed to have the water closets at the school house cleaned up."

The Marshal finally just said "no." A new Marshal was elected at the next meeting.

NINETEENTH CENTURY MISCELLANY

House-to-house salesmen were required to have a license. The Town Marshal was instructed to build an animal pound at "a convenient location at a cost not exceeding $10." Feeding a prisoner for seven days cost $4.20. Salary for 19 days of street work was $19. Finally, New Smyrna tried its hand at promotional advertising with "a page of descriptive matter of New Smyrna and a page of illustration of such cuts as the town might furnish for four months in *Sun Lands* for the sum of $15."

NEW STREET LAMPS BROKEN

Yet another duty of the Town Marshal was lighting and extinguishing the gas street lights. New Smyrna's first street lamps were 18 "Sun Vapor Street Lamps" purchased from the City of Jacksonville on May 21, 1895. In November 1899 the Street Lamp Committee was told to order 24 more lamps. Within four months of their installation, three lamps on Hillsborough Street and one on Canal Street were mysteriously broken.

"I cannot say how these lamps have been broken, but if it has been the custom for the Marshal to pay for lamps that have been broken, I want to pay for these or replace them, as the Council may see fit," Town Marshal W.S. Abbott reported on April 3, 1900.

YOU BREAK IT, YOU FIX IT

Road repair was a major expense by 1904; the city passed an ordinance requiring heavy "log cars, timber carts or turpentine carts shall keep the portions of streets used by them in good repair." Also, they "shall repair any damage done without delay." Offenders faced a $50 fine or 10 days in jail.

VOTING FRAUD—WELL, ONE VOTE....

After the 1902 election on July 7th, "the name of D.J. Bell was ordered stricken from the registration lists owing to the irregularity of its getting on the list."

YOU CAN'T WHIP A DROWNED HORSE

J.W. Wilson of Oak Hill claimed $75 damages for his horse which drowned "while trying to cross a bridge which he supposes belongs to the town."

Councilman T.J. Murray decided to solve the mystery by examining records in DeLand to determine whether the bridge was within the town limits. At the December 2, 1902 meeting he reported the bridge "was probably within the town limits."

The council didn't meet him halfway. They allowed $25 damages, which Wilson refused "saying he would have the $75 or nothing [these last two words are marked through in the original minutes] or bring suit."

Upon reflection of two months, this tough talk eventually led to a $25 settlement on February 3, 1903.

TOWN MARSHAL TROUBLES AGAIN

Mayor C.Y. Hesse told fellow council members he had "suspended the town Marshal for neglect of duty in allowing crossing of the street to be blocked from early one morning until after noon of next day, and also for having failed to report L.C. Chisholm [the town barber] for riding a bicycle without a light."

The rest of the councilmen thought otherwise and reinstated the Marshal with full pay at their February 3, 1903 meeting. On May 11th the Town Marshal J.F. Cannova resigned.

TELEPHONES RING IN NEW SMYRNA

Earliest discussion of a telephone franchise in New Smyrna began in 1897. Town Clerk J.P. Turner petitioned the City Council for erecting "poles and electrical apparatus necessary to construct and maintain a telephone exchange" in 1902. Finally, the New Smyrna Telephone Company was granted the right to establish a telephone exchange on April 5, 1904.

The 30-year franchise included the stipulation that "the rental of said telephones not to exceed $24 annum to any customer."

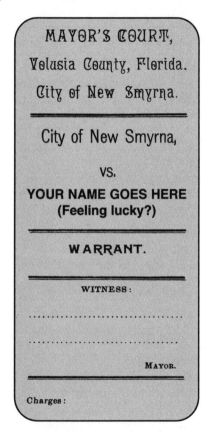

MAYOR'S COURT,
Volusia County, Florida.
City of New Smyrna.

City of New Smyrna,

vs.

YOUR NAME GOES HERE
(Feeling lucky?)

WARRANT.

WITNESS:

....

....

MAYOR.

Charges:

These excerpts were transcribed from New Smyrna's first police docket. It is a revealing chronology of *fin-de-siecle* and early 20th century crime.

Nothing's new about crime. Since crime increases with population, the problem is passed from one generation to another like a hot potato. So it goes...and grows.

There were more simple times, when New Smyrna really was a hideaway city—when it took 26 votes to elect the first mayor in 1887. Still, there were law and order concerns.

Here are the crimes that made the police docket beginning over a century ago. Welcome to the saga of the wild, wild Florida East Coast.

OUR FIRST RECORDED CRIME IS ASSAULT AND BATTERY

Wiley Jenkins holds the dubious honor of being the first entry in New Smyrna's leather bound police docket books. He was arrested by Town Marshal William Laurcey for assault and battery on February 18, 1889.

Jenkins was "sentenced to pay a fine of $10 and costs or to hard labor for ten days and be committed to the custody of the marshal until the fine is paid or the labor performed," ruled Mayor B.J. Skipper.

Court costs were $6.39, with $1.79 going to the mayor and the rest going to the marshal.

FOUL MOUTH BECOMES EMBARRASSINGLY POPULAR

"Disturbing the peace and using abusive language" got Charles King arrested in September 1889. King pleaded not guilty, but it didn't do any good. He was fined $5...big money for bad words.

By 1901 "swearing in the streets" was reduced to a $1 fine. When the price of foul mouth went down, swearing saw a dramatic rise. Five incidents were recorded that year.

DRUNKS DELUGE THE DOCKET

Probably the most recurrent entry in the dockets concerns drunks. Drinking has always been popular in New Smyrna—possibly due to its salty environment.

Charges of "drunk on the streets" and the more dangerous "drunk and asleep on the streets" brought $1 fines in 1891.

The passive drunk faded. Alarming increases in "disturbing the peace" and "drunk and disorderly" charges were evidenced. To combat this ever rising drunken tide, fines levied against tipsy townsmen leaped to $10 per offense by 1905.

Drunks either become docile or violent when they're flying three sheets to the wind. "Shooting in the streets" and "concealed weapons" accompany some of these drunk charges. That was a big $25 fine in 1891.

However, your absolute best value for rowdiness was brawling. The fine was just a dollar a fight.

HAVE YOU STOPPED BEATING YOUR WIFE?

In the days before liberated women—long before they became advertising sex symbols or even had the right to vote—women who ran amuck with their husbands were beaten sometimes.

Though this was never officially sanctioned, a man charged with "whipping his wife" was fined $2.50 in 1902. Three years later the fine quadrupled to $10.

However, by 1908 the minimum ante for "beating his wife," "whipping his wife" or the alarming "whipping and burning his wife" brought fines of $25 apiece.

There *was* a reduced $10 fine for one incidence of wife beating in 1908. Perhaps the mayor thought the wife deserved at least some punishment.

BICYCLE LAW CREATES INSTANT CRIMINALS

With a stroke of the legal pen, criminals can be created. An ordinance was passed in 1895 requiring all bicycles to be equipped with lights and bells. Lights you can understand, but bells? Why not yell?

Naturally, every new law needs someone to use for an example. Harry Galbreath was the first offender to be apprehended. Hapless Harry was "reiding bycle with out leight." The Mayor's Court couldn't spell worth spit that day, but it certainly knew how to collect a two-dollar fine.

Bicycles were the rage in the 1890's. It's no surprise this particular ordinance was immensely profitable and therefore vigorously enforced.

Unlike our modern notions about fine and forfeiture, the quantity of offenders eventually led to a discount. By 1901 the fine was dropped to a dollar. Ding, ding!

SEX CRIME POTPOURRI

It may be commonplace today, but in 1905 a couple "illegally living together" was fined $10 each.

Pornography arrived in New Smyrna in 1908, when a man was arrested for "selling and exhibiting nude pictures." The fine was $25 or 30 days on the street crew.

Adultery cost $10 in 1912. The man was sent to a "detention camp" for an unspecified length of time.

MEET OUR FIRST RECKLESS DRIVERS

J.C. Turner was the first New Smyrnan to be apprehended for "reckless driving of an automobile." This momentous event occurred in August 1912. It also proved to be the first case of automobile recidivism. A year later Turner was picked up for "failing to sound horn at street corner."

The first recorded incidence of "reckless driving of a motorcycle" was in 1911. Born-to-be-wild motorcyclist Barry Lopez was fined one dollar.

MISCELLANEOUS CRIMES WORTHY OF MENTION

Dr. J.B. Greenwood was surprised when he found himself in Mayor's Court charged with "refusal to pay a special license tax."

Try as Dr. Greenwood might, he couldn't beat City Hall. He was fined $5. It would be interesting to see the good doctor's reaction to licensing, insurance policies, captial gains, and income taxes today.

E.J. Moore was found guilty of "setting his dogs on a bunch of hogs that P.J. McCarthy had in his possession and using profane language within the city limits." No details were recorded concerning the punishment.

Who can tame the tongue? The "use of profane and indecent language and making improper proposals" to two young women landed a budding Don Juan a "$20 fine or 15 days labor on the streets."

"Singing of an indecent song" got Henry Thompson a $10 fine in 1912, even though he pleaded not guilty. Too bad the name of that catchy tune was not recorded.

Finally, the most enigmatic charge of them all occurs in the record during 1906.

Today it's fashionable to be flashy and bad...super bad. Some folks strive for this reputation, using rough language and outrageous fashions, carrying knives or guns, and generally showing off. You know, trying to convince others how tough they are.

Such conduct is nearly a century old. A man was charged with "very bad conduct." Further details don't exist, but he was fined a very fashionable $10.

LEFT: Welcome to New Smyrna. If you were traveling on the Dixie Highway—US #1—in 1927, these "city gates" would have greeted you at our northern city limits.

By 1930 New Smyrna was a busy town of almost 4,200. The Dixie Highway was widened. The "city gates," which resembled those of St. Augustine, were replaced by an illuminated sign in the Thirties.

RIGHT: This new sign seemed to increase accidents, say old timers. It seems the lights drew night-time drivers like mosquitoes.

Both entrances were located in the median strip just south of what is today the Regions Bank, 900 North Dixie Freeway. The highway was four-laned in 1957.

"To Ocean Beach 1 Mile" is pure fiction. Even a bird would have to fly two miles.

Volusia County's first school was located near the future site of the New Smyrna Historical Museum, 120 Sams Avenue. No bond issue was needed in 1872; a petition requested public donations of money, labor or materials. As a result, our first school cost $42.

F.W. Sams, owner of the Ocean House hotel, brought Miss Delia Stowe from Massachusetts to serve as governess for his children. She became Volusia County's first teacher.

The school year was three to six months, six hours a day. Curriculum included reading, writing, arithmetic, spelling, history, and geography. Two days each week were spent on needlework or farming.

LEFT: New Smyrna's second school was built in 1885 on the corner of Canal and Live Oak streets, today the site of Christmas Tree Park. After 1901, the two-story school became a photographic studio, "Conrad's Kodak Place."

The unique "tree in the street" at the left of this photo remained until the 1950's. It was located on the east side of today's Bob's Exxon Service Station, 151 Canal Street.

RIGHT: The Mary Avenue school opened in 1901. By all appearances, recess was a favorite subject in more than one century. Evidenced in this photo, hats were the fashion statement of the day.

The Mary Avenue facility served up to the sixth grade level until 1903. Soon after, seventh and eighth grades were added. By 1912 high school grades had been included.

New Smyrna had humble beginnings. The town valued education. After all, the task was to learn the basics, not to sponsor some frivolous fashion show.

In 1900 the school dress code accommodated bare feet. What would they have thought of today's $100 designer gym shoes?

Meet Room #1 on the front steps of the Mary Avenue School. If there ever was attention deficit, it was because the school was built next to the FEC Railway tracks. Without any help from students, classes were disrupted every time a train passed through town.

The Mary Avenue School was replaced in 1916 by the Faulkner Street School, two blocks east of the tracks.

RIGHT: You are looking toward the river. The East Coast Bargain House is now surveyor Dan Corey's office, 300 Canal Street. In 1907 the street was a mix of commercial buildings and family residences. The Turnbull Canal is to the left; one bridge can be seen in the foreground. When the canal was covered by the north sidewalk in 1924, the street evolved into a traditional business district.

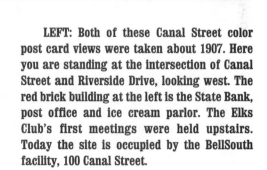

LEFT: Both of these Canal Street color post card views were taken about 1907. Here you are standing at the intersection of Canal Street and Riverside Drive, looking west. The red brick building at the left is the State Bank, post office and ice cream parlor. The Elks Club's first meetings were held upstairs. Today the site is occupied by the BellSouth facility, 100 Canal Street.

RIGHT: Saturday was market day on Canal Street in 1931. There were at least five different groceries and butcher shops to visit on the street. This view looks east from the intersection of North Orange Street. Parking spaces were painted as parallel, but creative New Smyrnans must have liked diagonal parking better. Daytona Beach photographer Harry Lesesne is standing at the lower left.

LEFT: More than a decade later, here's the intersection of Canal and Magnolia streets. Why the stoplight? Magnolia was the original US #1; it went west on Canal and then up North Orange Street. Davis Corner Store (right) was a popular drug store soda fountain hangout and employer of the town's teenagers. Also, after a decade of practice, townspeople seem to have mastered the art of parallel parking.

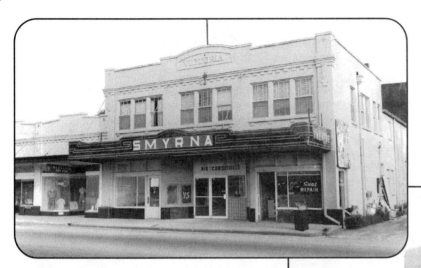

LEFT: Victoria Theater, named in honor of pioneer settler Victoria Sheldon, opened its 554-seat facility in 1923. Tom Mix in "Soft Boiled" was featured. Later, it became the air-conditioned Smyrna Theater. Who knows how many teenage romances began here? Little Drug Company, founded in 1920, moved into the building in 1965 and remains today at 412 Canal Street. (Photo by Clyde Savey)

RIGHT: Built in 1925, the old post office building, 120 Sams Avenue, will become the New Smyrna Historical Museum, opening during 2002. From its first meeting in July 1982, the Southeast Volusia Historical Society, Inc. has progressed rapidly. Period displays, gift and book shop, research library, and more will be featured. Learn more in the society's *Mosqueto News* or web site at www.sevhs.org.

New Smyrna held the continental US record for "Most Rainfall in 24 Hours" for years, a dubious record now claimed by Yankeetown, Florida. After all, no tourism campaign can sell rainy vacation days. A.B. Nordman, who lived north of the Municipal Airport, measured 23.22 inches in 18 hours on October 9-10, 1924. The seven-day total was 35.33 inches. "The man or woman who didn't get soaked during those days was not considered a good citizen," the *New Smyrna News* scolded citizens who didn't offer assistance to their beleagured city. The canopy at the left is 223 Canal Street, today the Sun Service Center, looking east. Classes were cancelled at the Faulkner Street School. Below, Mission Road was flooded up to your axles.

TOP LEFT: New Smyrna's oldest hotel began as Ora Carpenter's tavern, built in 1856-57. Rebuilt after the 1863 Union bombardment, it was a popular tourist destination. The hotel was demolished in the 1940's and is presently the site of the County Courthouse Annex, 126 North Riverside Drive.

ABOVE: The Rio Vista Hotel, 1200 South Riverside Drive, opened in 1916 and featured the first elevator in town. Known as The Gordon in the Twenties, then the New Smyrna Hotel in the Thirties, it became the Indian River Lodge in 1963.

LEFT: Alba Court, 115 Washington Street, opened in 1906. Its 26 rooms surrounded a three-story atrium. It had steam heat and a gas generating plant to provide gas lighting. Each room got plumbing in 1917. Rates were "$3 and up. Special by week."

RIGHT: Here's a perfect day for sailing on the Indian River North, captured forever from the 1920's. This view is along South Riverside Drive, then called Hillsboro (Hillsborough) Street. Add a bulkhead, dredge and fill, and you would recognize this site today as beautiful Riverside Park in the shadow of the high-rise South Causeway bridge.

Indian River Steamer Swan, New Smyrna,

LEFT: The Intracoastal Waterway was the fastest and easiest means of travel in 1900. The first automobile to drive the sand road between New Smyrna to Daytona in 1904 took over an hour each way. The stern-wheeler *Swan* was 156 feet long, 34 feet wide and 5 feet deep. Built in Jacksonville in 1904, it was a common sight on the Halifax and Indian River North, difficult to miss at 371 gross tons.

THE NORTH BRIDGE CAME FIRST

A bridge raising of the George E. Musson Bridge opened in 1997 can still slow traffic, but before 1892 you would have taken a ferry across the Indian River North to Flagler Avenue.

The Connor Bridge was reopened on March 4, 1894, after the first bridge built in 1892 had been destroyed by a hurricane. Palmetto logs were jetted down for pilings by Ballough Bros., Daytona Beach contractors.

The causeway roadbed was laid by wheelbarrow. The bridge was almost 15 feet wide, barely allowing two carriages to pass.

Incorporated by Washington E. Connor, the New Smyrna Bridge and Investment Company was formed with $15,000 capital. Eighteen days after its opening, receipts showed a 10% return on the investment.

By 1923 this private toll bridge needed repairs, revenue was down, and there was talk of a competing South Bridge. Connor proposed deeding the free public Connor Library to the city as a gift if the county would purchase the bridge.

Since 1901 Connor had financed the library and paid its librarian. The county acquired the Connor Bridge in 1925 after the state approved $32,500 for its purchase.

1900

1925

1915

1937

RIGHT: The Austin Bros. Bridge Company of Atlanta, Georgia, was selected to build the South Bridge "with draw and toll house not to exceed $100,000." Opened in 1925, 45,000 cubic yards of fill were necessary to create the South Causeway. Youngsters 50 years ago will recall the disturbing noises made while crossing the South Bridge...the sound of loose boards and the prospect of certain doom!

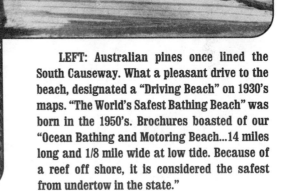

SOUTH BRIDGE

LEFT: Australian pines once lined the South Causeway. What a pleasant drive to the beach, designated a "Driving Beach" on 1930's maps. "The World's Safest Bathing Beach" was born in the 1950's. Brochures boasted of our "Ocean Bathing and Motoring Beach...14 miles long and 1/8 mile wide at low tide. Because of a reef off shore, it is considered the safest from undertow in the state."

Welcome to quaint Coronado Beach, self-proclaimed "The World's Safest Beach." The town also boasted of 31 cottages, two stores, two livery stables, and a 40-room hotel by 1893. Cottages cost between $400 to $1,600.

This 1944 photo shows the archway and bridge tender's house in front of the Riverview Hotel. In 1937, New Smyrna added "Beach" to its name without owning any oceanfront property. Nine years later it annexed Coronado Beach.

CORONADO BEACH: OUR FORGOTTEN COMMUNITY

"Beach" is the only word that even suggests Coronado Beach, once a separate community annexed by New Smyrna on April 1, 1946. The community was founded on our beachside as early as 1885 by Foster G. Austin and was incorporated in 1925.

As editor of the *Observer* newspaper, I interviewed the last mayor of Coronado Beach, J.G. Schauwecker. He had spent six years on the Coronado Council, and two years as Mayor and Municipal Judge before the town was annexed by New Smyrna Beach.

Here's his story in 1974 as he sat in his favorite rocking chair and smoked a hand-rolled cigarette:

◆ Annexation (1946) passed by 36 votes. "There were probably 1,000 people over here; maybe 500 were registered voters."

◆ "This little town developed tremendously. Beach crowds, even then, were tremendous. We budgeted $500 one summer for lifeguards—half a dozen of them. We had two drownings; I remember one of them: his name was Ivory Brown."

◆ "Councilmen never got a nickel. At one time, they

gave free water over here at the council meetings, but they quit that. Cost too much. We didn't have a fire department and we had some big fires over here, too. We had our own police force: two or three men and a part-time officer. Water and electric for Coronado came from New Smyrna. Actually, we gave the town away to get New Smyrna water over here."

◆ Coronado Elementary School was located behind today's Coronado Beach Club House on Flagler Avenue.

◆ "There was one year when I made only one arrest. It was two speeding cars. There were five boys in each car. I was municipal judge then, too. I fined them $15 in each car. Their lawyer came late, but they got off easy. That's how well the town was managed."

◆ After annexation, Coronado Beach turned its records over to New Smyrna: "We had a debt service of $32,000 to $34,000. That's all we owed. The town had a break-even budget."

◆ "We were far ahead of the other side [New Smyrna], growing by leaps and bounds. They tried for 20 years to take the town over—unsuccessfully. Well, we didn't have water; there was danger of contagion and disease. It was the struggle of a small community trying to live. New Smyrna has taken taxes out and put very little back in."

Old Coronado of the 1890s is today's Hill Street area.

Coronado Beach was the name given Foster G. Austin's homestead in 1885. The first development was several beachside cottages about a mile south of Flagler Avenue. This later came to be known as "Old Coronado." Some claim Austin named this Florida community in honor of his California hometown, Coronado Beach.

According to the Coronado (California) Visitors Bureau, the land directly across from San Diego, which would become Coronado Beach, was "a barren peninsula whose chief population was jack-rabbits until it was purchased in 1885 by Elisha S. Babcock, Jr. and Hampton L. Story."

RIVER VIEW HOTEL

ACROSS THE INDIAN RIVER FROM NEW SMYRNA

FRED H. TRYON, PROP.

Without a sense of history, we tend to forget our origins. The Riverview Hotel began as a two-story hunting and fishing lodge built by Captain S.H. Barber in 1885. Barber was the Coronado Beach bridge tender and a part-time carpenter. In 1904 he and builder John Vrooman jacked up the existing building to serve as the second and third stories, building a new lobby and dining room underneath. The name was changed from "Barber House" to "River View Hotel" in 1924.

Fred Tryon purchased the hotel in 1936. No stranger to this business, Tryon had been head chef at the Alcazar Hotel in St. Augustine before moving to New Smyrna. He managed the River View Hotel during 1930-31, as well as others in this area before deciding to buy it in 1936. Tryon was responsible for the west wing and adding individual bathrooms and steam heat. The hotel (like many others) was open in the winter and closed in the summer until World War II, when local Coast Guardsmen who patrolled the beach stayed there.

Tryon died in 1954; his daughters, Babe Paxton and Dorothy "Do" Miller, and son-in-law Richard Paxton, ran the hotel. Declining hotel occupancy led to its use in the 1970's as a youth hostel. The building suffered neglect; its unpainted condition earned it the nickname "The Gray Ghost." Some called for its demolition while others began a bumper sticker campaign: "Quaint—Not Paint." Finally, fire code violations brought its closing in 1980.

The future looked dim until John Spang of Winter Park bought the Riverview properties in March 1984 for $520,000. His extensive renovation included adding a swimming pool and building a fine restaurant, Riverview Charlie's. The hotel became a show place with a new lease on life a century later.

Jim and Christa Kelsey, former owners of the Faro Blanco Marine Resort in Marathon, Florida, purchased the property in November 1990. The Kelseys have made further renovations and improvements, including Victorian gingerbread trim, new storm windows, partitioned verandas, and the addition of a well-stocked, quaint little gift shop.

1903

1920's

1905

1937

HERE LIES CHARLES DUMMETT IN THE MIDDLE OF THE STREET

"Sacred to the Memory of Charles Dummett, Born August 18, 1844 – Died April 23, 1860."

Young Charles Dummett's final resting place could go unnoticed by most beachside residents and visitors.

Charles' father Douglas Dummett was in the sugar business. He rose to fame by commanding the volunteer "Mosquito Roarers" during the Second Seminole War.

Later he became Peace Justice for the county, first Collector of Customs for the Port of New Smyrna, and budded sweet oranges found in Turnbull Hammock (south of New Smyrna) to establish the famous Dummett citrus grove on Merritt Island. This strain was the beginning of our world famous Indian River citrus.

Douglas Dummett married the daughter of a socially prominent family, but she promptly deserted him for another. Dummett moved to New Smyrna and built a home on an Indian mound which he named Mt. Pleasant. The mound once stood on South Indian River Road.

Dummett married a young, black slave girl, Anna, for his second wife. They had three daughters and a son, Charles, who was born in 1844. The boy was sent to a Northern school for his education.

Charles was home from school in April 1860. He and a friend were hunting near Mt. Pleasant when Charles tripped and his gun discharged. He was killed instantly. Dummett buried his son where he fell.

When Mt. Pleasant was bulldozed for residential development during the 1960's, it was named Canova Drive. Earlier, entertainer Judy Canova's plans for a trailer park had been refused by the city. To avoid legal difficulties of moving the grave, developers left the sarcophagus. Thus the pavement on Canova Drive is divided—leaving a grave in the middle of the street.

RIGHT: Flagler Avenue is narrow because it started out that way. The four-story Atlantic House was built in 1896 by William Newell from New York. It sat east of South Atlantic Avenue near the Flagler ramp parking lot. Newell's cottage with a three-sided veranda (far right) is now Nichols Surf Shop, 411 Flagler Avenue. Its blueprints came from the mail-order house of Sears and Roebuck and Co., "Cheapest Supply House on Earth."

LEFT: The Atlantic House was our first oceanfront hotel. It was a popular social center; dancing to the music of Holly's orchestra was popular on Saturday nights. On April 22, 1916, it was destroyed by fire. No lives were lost because most of the winter visitors had already left. The first building on the right side of the street is currently The Flagler Tavern, 414 Flagler Avenue.

RIGHT: More frequent than hurricanes, northeasters visit New Smyrna every year. Our worst northeaster was October 3, 1947; it caused $500,000 damage. Beachfront cottages were turned upside down or washed away. The Casino, a popular eating, drinking and dancing establishment, was destroyed. It was built at the Flagler Avenue ramp, today occupied by the Flagler parking lot.

LEFT: A decade later, here is a perfect blue-sky day with friendly cumulus clouds. Enjoy the idyllic mid-Fifties at the Flagler Avenue ramp. Note the legendary "peanut tree" in the foreground. These provided shade—limited to your head or feet, but not both. Thank photographer Clyde Savey for capturing this fleeting beach moment for eternity with his 4x5 Speed Graphic camera.

"All New Smyrna children know how to fish."
– A.E. Dumble, artist, poet and author, 1904

Varieties of fish caught in New Smyrna according to *Where, When and How to Catch Fish on the East Coast of Florida* by William H. Gregg, 1902, include: Besougas, Black Bass, Sea Bass, Bladder-fish, Bluefish, Bream, Catfish, Cavalle, Channel Bass, Croaker, Drum, Flounder, Grouper, Gulf-fish, Jewfish, Ladyfish, Mullet, Moon-fish, Needle-fish, Mutton-fish (not the Pargo variety), Pigfish, Pilot-fish, Pompano, Porcupine-fish, Saw-fish, Sharks, Sheepshead, Sailor's Choice, Sea Robin, Sergeant-fish, Snappers (Mangrove, Gray and Rabirubia), Sand Conger, Skate, Spadefish, Spanish Mackerel, Tarpon, Spotted Sea Trout, Tripletail, Whiting, and Yellow Tail.

Below: Have a nice stingray day!

RIGHT: Beware of creatures of the deep! This giant manta ray is just the right stuff for bad dreams. These young anglers seem brave enough—at least on dry land in the daylight. Standing on the river bank at Florida Avenue about 1928 are (left to right): Charles Moore, Shirley Jones, Doris McCullough, Ronnie Moore, Mac McCullough, and Wilbur Jones.

LEFT: No darkroom hocus-pocus was involved in this photo. It is what it appears to be—a giant leatherback turtle, which can weight up to 1,000 pounds. Long ago, the high point of summer was turtle egging. These eggs made exceptionally moist pancakes and pound cakes. Caution! Today even disturbing turtles carries a heavy penalty. (Photo courtesy of Halifax Historical Society, Inc.)

Shades of Moby Dick! Nine whales (35-43 feet long) washed ashore on June 13, 1908, near the lighthouse. New Smyrna residents Frank Sams, Albert Moeller, Elmer Oliver, and Jerome Naley formed a company with John Pettigrew and Captain S. Bennett (once a New England whaler) of Daytona Beach. They were going into the lucrative whale oil extraction business.

Using the giant kettles from the historic Sugar Mill, they toiled over the boiling whale blubber. Perhaps they should have reviewed Herman Melville's classic whaling novel more closely. Each whale usually yielded about 45 barrels of valuable oil. Something went wrong; instead, they created a city-wide stench. Smaller pieces of whale were hauled out to the Inlet, but the remaining carcasses required dynamiting. Alas, the way of all easy-money schemes!

Attention everyone: Pop is peeved. He really doesn't want your comments or advice. Just shut up and sit down. This still happens today. The solution is $85 for a tow truck. (Photo courtesy of the Halifax Historical Society, Inc.)

"There is no new thing under the sun." – Ecclesiastes 1:9 Suddenly you realize that your generation didn't invent surfing along New Smyrna's beach. Truth be told, your grandparents or great-grandparents probably did. Here's photographic proof.

In its infancy, this new surf sport might have caused trouble at home, though. Don't you imagine mothers of the 1920's wondered why their ironing boards were frequently missing? Or why they were always damp when finally found?

1890's   Photo by E.G. Harris

1904

1900

The first car was driven on New Smyrna's beach about 1904. Mrs. George Saxon (Harris Saxon's mother) is seated at the right rear. Whether you're in a horse and buggy, horseless carriage or on a bicycle, it has always been a beach tradition to cruise—to see and to be seen.

In recent history, protection of turtle nesting sites has led to some driving restrictions. Daytona Beach has created car-free zones, mostly benefiting exclusive oceanfront properties. Early photos testify to the public ownership of our shoreline, long before condominiums cast shadows on the beach.

In fact, an early survey of Hill Street shows the beach is platted as a road—appropriately called "Ocean Street."

Wrecked here

EARLY WRECKS ALONG THE SHORES OF NEW SMYRNA

Whatever washed ashore was important to New Smyrna's early families. Beachcombing after storms was a community affair. Wrecks contributed food, clothing, knickknacks, and building material—even a survivor or two who eventually became residents. Here are a few.

1774: William Bartram's map in *Travels of William Bartram* notes "Wrecked here" of his vessel in the vicinity of today's Third Avenue beach ramp.

1779: A privateer wrecked north of the Inlet. The crew of 50 was taken prisoner and sent to St. Augustine.

1788: Mosquito Bar claimed the *Betsy*, a British ship commanded by Captain Grant, from Nassau. This same ship had carried 120 Turnbull colonists to New Smyrna 20 years earlier.

1847: The *Narragansett* was a 576-ton sidewheel steamer, bound for New Orleans from New York. It wrecked on the north side of the Inlet on October 28, 1847.

Shortly thereafter, the *Roxanna* and the *Ocean* followed, shown on the 1851 US Coast Survey. The *Roxanna* ran aground on the north peninsula, while the *Ocean* lodged on a sand bar at the confluence of the Halifax River, Inlet and Hillsborough River (renamed Indian River North in 1901).

1858: About 100 miles off the coast, the *Dido* started leaking. On New Year's Day she made Mosquito Inlet and anchored inside the outer bar. Her captain drowned.

1860: On November 13, the schooner *Manfred* under Captain Guion sank at New Smyrna.

During The War Between the States the *Lavina R,* a former African slaver, washed ashore at Miller Boardwalk (today the Crawford Road beach approach). The ship had been running the blockade to Nassau with a cargo of turpentine.

The *Ladona* wrecked shortly afterwards, en route to New Orleans from New York. It provided a rich supply of beach booty. Beachcombers who came barefoot and ragged pranced away with patent leather slippers and store-made clothes designed for the dandies of New Orleans. Some combers mistook the fancy fruits made of soap for real, took a big bite, and threw them back.

One woodsman picked up a Turkish towel embedded in the sand and proclaimed, "Wa'al thet ship had more tripe aboard'en I ever seen in my life."

1865: The *Villanfranco* was bound for New York, sprang a leak and sank. The ship and cargo of sugar and molasses were lost in latitude 29°. (Ponce de Leon Inlet is 29.072° N.) All hands were saved.

Late 1860's: The sloop *Martha* capsized in a squall off Ponce de Leon Inlet. Two lives were lost. The cargo of salt mullet was salvaged.

1871: The schooner *Nellie Burgess* was driven ashore on the Inlet bar during a gale in November. The ship was a total loss.

1878: The Central American schooner *Pinta* wrecked four miles south of the Inlet during a September hurricane. Its cargo of 150,000 coconuts spread for miles. Always thrifty, some folks pressed out the oil and used it for cooking. An Oak Hill resident named Geiger reportedly ate so many coconuts he died.

"There's where I dropped some money," mused Captain R.S. Sheldon, who bid $150 for the cargo and won. Before he could salvage all the nuts, the sun split many of them. Next, a yellow fever epidemic at Jacksonville closed that market. A few of Sheldon's coconuts were finally sold, shipped inland by wagon.

1879: In February, the *Belle of Texas,* a flat bottomed Mississippi side wheeler, was battered against the beach two miles north of Turtle Mound.

Although the ship was a total loss, the crew came ashore. The trail made across the river at that point is still called the Belle-of-Texas Trail.

Also in 1879 the *Ida Simpson* wrecked and deposited resident Peter Paul. Drifting in at New Smyrna on this schooner's wrecked timbers, Paul has remained ever since. A sailor since boyhood, Paul had quit his post on the ill-fated *Vera Cruz* just before its final voyage in August 1880 (see page 122).

He became a mate on the *Ida Simpson* instead. "I didn't come to New Smyrna," said Paul. "The good Lord put me here and I stayed, figuring He knew best."

1880: *The Fitch* was driven ashore at Detwiler's Pavilion. Gustavus Spleiss was washed ashore; he was picked up by Captain R.S. Sheldon and taken home. Spleiss liked his treatment and stayed in New Smyrna, becoming the community's first undertaker.

Spleiss was born in Danzig, Germany, and at the age of 16 went to sea for 21 years.

"In 1880 he was wrecked off this coast and the young man was washed ashore on a piece of wreckage, landing on the beach February 3, 1880. He was so impressed with the natural beauty of this section he decided to remain and has made his home here since that time," reported the *New Smyrna News* obituary of January 16, 1914.

1880: While coastal residents surveyed their own hurricane damage, the *City of Vera Cruz* had broken in half and sunk 30 miles east of the Inlet on August 29. Debris and bodies washed ashore from St. Augustine to Cape Canaveral.

Then the first survivor came ashore at Ormond with the awful story. En route from New York to Mexico, the ship had been caught in a hurricane. Of the 128 passengers, 15 came ashore at Port Orange; several other small groups came ashore alive nearby. Local settlers just north of Ormond reported burying "67 bodies in one large pit dug back of the first row of dunes."

1896: The 75-ton Mexican *Steam Tug of Tabasco* sank off Mosquito Bank on May 25 at 11:00 a.m. The ship was a total loss.

1897: On New Year's Day, the steamer *Commodore* sank about 12 miles off Daytona Beach. It was carrying munitions to Cubans fighting for independence from Spain. Surviving this wreck is recorded in an exceptional short story, "The Open Boat," by Stephen Crane, then a *New York Press* correspondent. Crane and three other men spent 30 hours in a lifeboat before reaching shore.

The 80-ton shrimp trawler *Mary M* from Bridgeport, Connecticut, ran aground a mile from the lighthouse in November 1936. The captain and crew camped out on the beach, using their canvas sails for tents. Their entire catch was lost; a donation was taken up. The whole town became caught up in this three-week rescue. First, the bow was jacked up and rollers placed underneath. The plan was to pull the ship out to sea using 12-inch hawsers. Onlookers cheered whenever the boat moved. Aided by the Coast Guard and 200 townsfolk, a tearful Captain William Metzger and crew were afloat again. They waved their hats farewell as the *Mary M* sounded her whistle.

This shipwreck was briefly uncovered by a northeaster in March 1967. It is still located south of the Pelican Condominium, 2401 South Atlantic Avenue. (Photo courtesy of Len Hays)

"PIECES OF EIGHT" are two-ounce coins, 99.3% silver

EVERYONE WANTS TO KNOW: WHERE IS THE TREASURE?

Sooner or later, someone will ask: Where is the treasure of New Smyrna hidden? Our mysterious coquina ruins and whispered history of the original colonists' suffering in the 1770's add to the effect.

If you listen long enough, you'll hear stories of old maps and buried treasure, payments by early residents made in Spanish coins, hunters who discovered silver ingots, and sunken treasure in Turnbull Bay. True or false? You might recall two of Mark Twain's adages: "No secret in a small town is more than 24 hours old" and "Never let the facts stand in the way of a good story."

What has been discovered includes Indian pottery, tools, bones, ballast stones, bronze ship nails, bottles, buttons, china, and coins from every era. Musketballs and cannonballs from the 1862 skirmish and 1863 bombardment of New Smyrna during The War Between the States have been found.

No doubt, the "real" treasure most of us dream about lies scattered on the ocean floor. The Spanish began their annual treasure ("plate") fleets in 1552 and continued for almost 200 years. Their usual course was from

Cartagena, Colombia; to Vera Cruz, Mexico; to Havana, Cuba; and up the Florida coast. Turtle Mound marked the turn east-northeast to Bermuda; then due east to the Azores. From there the treasure fleets followed the coast home to Cadiz, Spain.

Silver was abundant. Gold represented only 5% of the precious metals mined. Appropriately, the "Plate Fleet" derives its name from *plata*, Spanish for silver.

There was a marked decline in treasure fleet activity after 1648, coinciding with a decrease in New World silver production and increased pirate attacks. Between 1570-1599 there were 110 ships in the fleet. From 1670 to 1690, only 17 ships sailed.

Nearly 98% of the wrecks before 1825 sank in shallow waters, caught by treacherous reefs and shallows or sudden tropical storms. Early salvage workers were efficient; they recovered 90% of the treasure lost in depths of less that 50 feet.

The 1715 hurricane sank 11 of 12 treasure fleet galleons along the Florida East Coast. The fleet officially carried 6,486,066 pesos in gold and silver, plus an unrecorded amount of amethyst and jewelry.

Electronic beachcombers search for the elusive treasure of New Smyrna.

By 1719 when the Spanish stopped salvage work, more than 8.5 million pesos had been recovered, suggesting the crew was carrying a great deal of contraband treasure for themselves.

To date, seven of these 11 wrecks have been rediscovered by using high-technology proton magnetometers.

Other treasure fleets were similarly doomed. Seventeen of 22 galleons in the 1733 fleet were lost in a hurricane.

Shipwrecked crews who swam ashore usually sought the safety of St. Augustine. However, landing near (or south) of Cape Canaveral might have been worse than the ravages of the sea. Fierce cannibals—the Ais Indians—inhabited this region.

Occasionally a few coins or a small cache is discovered along the beach. These are probably castoffs of some shipwrecked soul who jettisoned his burden in the long and dangerous march to St. Augustine.

Centuries later, after a northeaster or unusually high tides, our beaches are dotted with treasure hunters and their expensive equipment. The hope against hope of effortless gain is truly historical.

FIRST LIGHTHOUSE NEVER SHINES

Territory of Florida planters and ship captains first petitioned Congress for a lighthouse in 1830. Four years later an $11,000 contract was awarded to build a 45-foot brick lighthouse and keeper's building on the south side of the inlet. A 12-foot dune was selected. Today its site would be in Smyrna Dunes Park on North Peninsula Drive.

The design featured eleven 14-inch reflectors, each reflector contained six ounces of pure silver. A copper dome enclosed the lamp assembly.

Although it was completed in February 1835, our first lighthouse was never lit because fuel oil was not delivered. In October a fierce gale destroyed the tender's house and undermined the tower. Seminole Indians burned New Smyrna and the lighthouse on December 28th. The structure slipped into the sea by April 1836.

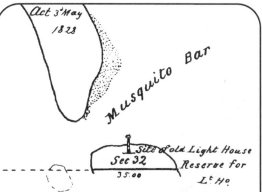

A.M. Randolph's survey of 1845 shows the site of our first lighthouse on the south peninsula.

Usual claims of shoddy workmanship, no plans, lack of supervision followed. No one mentioned the project was completed on time and over $3,500 under budget.

Lighthouse keeper William H. Williams, whose annual salary was $450, explained: "The reflectors of the lamps were lost; they were placed in a trunk in the dwelling house to prevent them from tarnishing as they were not in use—the dampness of the lighthouse damaging them very much."

The Indians took these reflectors during their rampage. In the Battle of Dunlawton (Port Orange), the Seminole chief Coacoochee (Wildcat) reportedly wore a reflector as a helmet or breastplate.

The outbreak of the Second Seminole War in 1835 halted any further work, although $7,000 was appropriated for changing the location to the north side of the inlet and building a second lighthouse. The funds were never spent. Instead, New Smyrna waited until 1883 when work was begun on the current lighthouse.

Late 1888—over 1.25 million bricks needed before completion.

PONCE DE LEON LIGHTHOUSE WAS COMMISSIONED IN 1887

Until 1887, most ships entering our inlet trusted to luck and a good local pilot. Mosquito Inlet (renamed Ponce de Leon Inlet in 1927) had a lengthy history and an unforgiving reputation of collecting wrecks.

Writer and engineer Francis Hopkinson Smith designed the lighthouse; the project cost $500,000. Begun in 1883, its 200,000-candlepower lamp began service on November 1, 1887.

The brick and granite structure rests securely on a 45-foot wide, 12-foot deep foundation. The lighthouse is 32 feet in diameter at its base and tapers to 12.5 feet at the top. Towering 175 feet, it is the nation's second tallest lighthouse. It can be seen for almost 20 miles.

Originally the lamp burned mineral oil and was a fixed navigational light. In 1933 it was converted to a 500-watt electric lamp and fitted with a revolving Fresnel lens. The lamp flashed six times every 26 seconds.

Early lighthouse tenders never needed to go duck hunting—ducks came to them. Migrating ducks would fly against the wire screen around the lamp and plummet to the ground. Once 64 ducks were picked up in four hours.

Due to increasing maintenance expense, the official lighthouse was moved to the US Coast Guard Station on the south peninsula in 1970—near the site of the original 1835 lighthouse.

Admission to this landmark is modest compared to the view from 140 feet on the gallery deck. Consider making this 203-step climb in the morning or in cool weather before the sun has heated the red brick structure.

Through the efforts of the Ponce de Leon Lighthouse Preservation Association, Inc., restoration was begun in 1972 to establish an historic monument and museum. In 1983 its beacon was restored, making it a functional navigational aid again.

Three original keepers' quarters have been restored, housing historical displays. A gift shop, video theatre, radio shack, pump house, and a 48-foot tugboat *F.D. Russell* are also featured. A playground, picnic tables, grills, and restrooms are nearby.

A full discussion of the lighthouse is contained in Thomas W. Taylor's *The Beacon of Mosquito Inlet: A History of the Ponce de Leon Lighthouse.*

For more information, contact: Ponce de Leon Lighthouse Preservation Association, Inc., 4931 South Peninsula Drive, Ponce Inlet, FL 32127. (386) 761-1821. Or visit the Association's web site: www.ponceinlet.org.

BIBLIOGRAPHY

Bailyn, Bernard. *Voyagers to the West: A Passage in the Peopling of America on the Eve of the Revolution.* 1986. New York, NY: Alfred A. Knopf.

Bockelman, Charles W. *Six Columns and Fort New Smyrna.* 1985. Daytona Beach, FL: Halifax Historical Society, Inc.

Butler, Amos W. 1917. "Observations on Some Shellmounds of the Eastern Coast of Florida." Proceedings, 19th International Congress of Americanists, pp. 104-107.

Carlson, Charlie. *The First Florida Cavalry Regiment C.S.A.* 1999. New Smyrna Beach, FL: Luthers Publishing.

Corse, Carita Doggett. 1919. *Dr. Andrew Turnbull and the New Smyrna Colony.* Facsimile reprint. New Smyrna Beach, FL: Luthers Publishing.

Dumble, A.E. 1904. *New Smyrna, Florida.* DeLand, FL: E.O. Painter.

Fitzgerald, T.E. 1937. *Volusia County, Past and Present.* Daytona Beach, FL: Observer Press.

Florida Anthropological Society. *Florida Archaeology: An Overview.* 1997. Tampa, FL.

Griffin, Patricia C. 1977. *Mullet on the Beach: The Minorcans of Florida, 1768-1788.* St. Augustine, FL: St. Augustine Historical Society.

Hubbell, Royal. 1906. *Ancient and Modern New Smyrna and Vicinity.* Annotated by Gary Luther, 1997. New Smyrna Beach, FL: Luthers Publishing.

Lowery, Woodbury. 1901. *The Spanish Settlements: 1513-1561.* New York, NY. The Knickerbocker Press.

Luther, Gary. *Bicentennial Extra.* 1976. New Smyrna Beach, FL: New Smyrna Beach Bicentennial Committee.

Luther, Gary. *History of New Smyrna, East Florida.* 1987. New Smyrna Beach, FL: Luthers Publishing.

Milanich, Jerald T. 1965. *Francisco Pareja's 1613 Confessionairo.* Tallahassee, FL: Florida Division of Archives.

Panagopoulos, E.P. 1966. *New Smyrna: An Eighteenth Century Greek Odyssey.* Gainesville, FL: University of Florida Press.

Quinn, Jane. 1975. *Minorcans of Florida: Their History and Heritage.* St. Augustine, FL: Mission Press.

Rasico, Philip D. 1990. *The Minorcans of Florida: Their History, Language, and Culture.* New Smyrna Beach, FL: Luthers Publishing.

Roselli, Bruno. 1940. *The Italians in Colonial Florida.* DeLand, FL: Drew Press.

Rutherford, Robert E. 1952. *Settlers from Connecticut in Spanish Florida. Letters of Ambrose Hull and Stella Hall Hull. 1804-1806 and 1808-1816.* Florida Historical Quarterly.

Siebert, William Henry. 1929. *Loyalists in East Florida, 1774-1785.* DeLand, FL: Florida Historical Society.

Sweett, Zelia Wilson, and J.C. Marsden. 1925. *New Smyrna, Florida: Its History and Antiquities.* DeLand, FL: E.O. Painter.

Sweett, Zelia Wilson. *New Smyrna, Florida in the Civil War.* 1963. Volusia County Historical Commission.

Weeks, Robert H. *New Smyrna, Volusia County, Florida: The Land of Flowers.* 1905. Facsimile reprint. New Smyrna Beach, FL: Luthers Publishing.

WPA Florida Writers' Project. *The Spanish Missions of Florida.* 1940. Reprint. New Smyrna Beach, FL: Luthers Publishing.

Every Florida story needs a gator.